Business and Commerce Workshop

Contents

Before you start

1 Which of these statements do you agree with?

1 Work is the most important thing in life.
2 Work is just a way to get money so you can do the things you enjoy.

Reading

2 Read what three people say about their jobs. Complete the chart with notes on the good and bad things about Anna's, Tony's, and Erika's jobs.

Anna, 18

'I work in a factory. My working hours are 8.00 a.m. to 5.00 p.m., Monday to Friday. I have a one-hour lunch break at 12.30. The routine is the same every day. My job is very boring but the pay is quite good. My colleagues and I don't really talk to each other, but I have a lot of friends outside work. My job is just a way to earn money.'

Tony, 23

'I'm a computer programmer. I work a 40-hour week. We have flexible hours so I can start and finish when I want. If we are very busy then I work overtime – I get paid extra for this. There are always problems to solve. This can be difficult, but it can also be quite creative. I earn a good salary, but my job doesn't rule my life. I like to do different things in my free time.'

Erika, 25

'I'm a doctor in a large hospital. I work very long hours - 60 or 70 hours a week - often in the evenings and at weekends. The work is really interesting but it can also be quite stressful. I love my job and my colleagues are also my friends. I don't have time for a social life. When I get home, I'm too tired to do anything except have dinner and watch TV.'

	good things	bad things
Anna		
Tony		
Erika		

Vocabulary

3 Match the highlighted words in the quotes with the definitions (1–8).

1 the people you work with _____
2 the number of hours in the week you spend doing your job _____
3 the money you receive every month for the work you have done _____
4 the things you do, usually with other people, outside work _____
5 the time you have for eating in the middle of the working day _____
6 the time you spend at work after your normal working hours _____
7 a system where you can choose when to start and finish work _____
8 the usual order and way that you regularly do things _____

4 Complete the sentences (1–6) with an adjective from the box.

> boring ■ busy ■ difficult ■ creative
> ■ interesting ■ stressful

1 If we have too much work and not enough time, it can be quite _____.
2 In my job, I use my imagination and ideas a lot, so the work is _____.
3 I do the same thing every day – my job is _____.
4 There is so much to do at work that I'm always _____.
5 Sometimes my job is _____, but I would get bored if it was too easy.
6 My job is very _____ because I'm always learning new things.

Speaking

5 Work in pairs. Which of the jobs in Exercise 2 would you most like to have? Which would you least like to have? Tell your partner why.

Writing

6 Think of a job you would like, or would not like, to have. Write a short text about it, using the texts in Exercise 2 as models.

▶ *Get real*

Interview someone you know about their job, e.g. a relative or family friend. Ask them what they like and don't like about their job. Find out if they live to work or work to live. Prepare to tell the class about them, in English.

2 Jobs in an organization

Before you start

1 Think about the people who work in your school, e.g. the teachers, the administrators. What are they *responsible for*? Who are they *responsible to*?

Reading

2 Read the text about some of the people in a film crew. Complete the diagram.

This is a fairly typical film set. On this film set, the director, John, is the boss. He's like the managing director of a company. He's responsible for making sure the film is made on time and to budget. The producer is really in charge of the business. In a normal company, he would be the chairperson. Our producer's name is Sam and he is responsible to the studio. They're the shareholders – the people who invest money in the film.

There are a lot of people involved in making a film. The camera operator is called Steve. He does all the filming and he's responsible to John. The sound recordist is Emma – she works closely with Steve. Her job is to record everything the actors say. Then there's Tony, the electrician. He looks after the equipment. Martin, the grip, organizes all the practical things and deals with any problems.

Finally, there's me. My name's Pat and I'm the assistant director. I help John, the director. I'm responsible for the rest of the crew, including Tony and Martin. My job is to make sure that everyone is in the right place at the right time and that they know what to do.

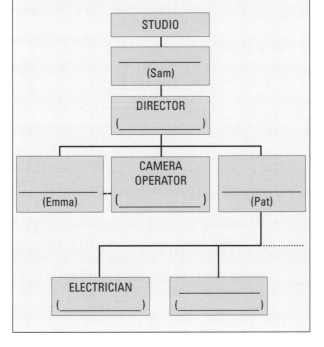

Vocabulary

3 Look at these phrases from the text. Use the Glossary or a dictionary to check any words you don't know. Then write them in your language.

Describing responsibility

My / Her job is to … _____
… is responsible for … _____
… is responsible to … _____
… in charge of … _____

Saying what someone does

… looks after … _____
… deals with … _____
… organizes … _____
… works closely with … _____

4 Complete the sentences (1–8) with a phrase from Exercise 3. Use each phrase only once.

1 The director tells the actors what to do and _____ any problems.
2 Martin _____ the practical things, like finding the right props.
3 I'm the camera operator. _____ record everything on film.
4 The director is _____ everything on the film set.
5 The electrician _____ the cameras, lights, and recording equipment.
6 Emma is _____ recording what people say.
7 The producer _____ the studio.
8 Pat _____ the director, John.

5 Complete 1–5 with words from the first paragraph.

1 The _____ is in charge of a company.
2 The _____ is money you have available to spend on a particular project.
3 The _____ is responsible for running a company.
4 To _____ is to put money into a business.
5 _____ put their money into a company.

Speaking

6 Work in pairs. Draw an organigram of an organization you know, e.g. your school or college. Explain it to another pair.

▶ ***Get real***

Talk to someone who works for a company or organization. Ask them how it is organized. Find out about the jobs and responsibilities of some of the people. Draw an organigram of the company and explain it to the class.

3 Parts of a company

Before you start

1 Look at the photos. Which departments of a company do they represent?

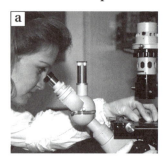   

Reading

2 Someone is giving a visitor a tour of a company. Read about the nine departments and match the pictures with four of the paragraphs. Then <u>underline</u> the names of all the departments.

OK, let's start here, in research and development, or R & D. This department is responsible for thinking of ideas for new products and finding ways to improve our existing products …

This department looks after our computer equipment. They deal with any problems. This is information technology, or IT …

Purchasing buys all the things we need to make our products. They talk to our suppliers and try to get the best price …

This is the main factory area, the production department. Here we make our products. It's the biggest part of the company …

Here in the finance department, they check how much the company is making and decide how much to spend. They also pay employees' salaries …

This department looks after the people who work here. Human resources is responsible for recruiting new employees, organizing training and helping with any problems …

Sales and marketing is very important. The marketing people think up the ideas for selling our products. The sales people go out and sell our products to our customers …

Customer services processes orders from customers. It organizes transportation, checks that customers have received their orders and deals with complaints …

Finally, distribution is responsible for transporting our products. They receive orders from customer services, and plan how and when to transport the products so the customers receive them at the right time …

Vocabulary

3 Match the names of the departments (1–9) with the phrases (a–i) to make a short description of each department.

1 Sales and marketing	a	transports the products.
2 Information technology	b	pays the salaries.
3 Customer services	c	sells the products.
4 Human resources	d	makes the products.
5 Purchasing	e	looks after the computers.
6 Production	f	thinks of ideas for new products.
7 R & D	g	recruits new staff.
8 Finance	h	processes orders from customers.
9 Distribution	i	buys parts from suppliers.

Speaking

4 Work in pairs to test each other. Take turns to ask questions about the different departments.

Which department pays the salaries?

5 Imagine you work in the human resources department of a manufacturing company. Give a short talk to some new employees.

- Decide what the company makes, e.g. bicycles, computers.
- Prepare the talk for some new employees. Explain what each department does. Don't write every word – just make notes.
- Give your talk to some other students.

▶ ### Get real

Use the Internet to find out about a large company, or visit a factory in your home town. Find out what the company makes, what departments it has and what they are called.

4 Nice to meet you

Before you start

1 How would you greet these people? What would you say? What would you do, e.g. shake hands, hug them?

- a friend you see often
- a relative you haven't seen for a while
- a visitor from another country

Reading

2 Anna (A) is meeting a visitor (B) at the airport. Match Anna's sentences with the replies.

A

1 Welcome to Poland.
2 Excuse me. Are you Mr Weiss?
3 Hello. I'm Anna. Nice to meet you.
4 Let me help you with your luggage.
5 Is this your first visit to Poland?
6 Did you have a good flight?

B

a Yes, thank you.
b No, I was here last year.
c Thank you. It's nice to be here.
d Yes, that's right.
e Thank you.
f Nice to meet you, too.

3 Put the conversation in a logical order.

2, _____

Vocabulary

4 Find and <u>underline</u> phrases in Exercise 2 that have a similar meaning to phrases 1–4 below.

1 How was your journey?
2 Pleased to meet you.
3 Have you been here before?
4 Can I give you a hand?

Speaking

5 Work in pairs. Read the dialogue in Exercise 2 aloud. Take turns to be A and B.

6 Look at these topics of conversation. Which ones are suitable when you meet someone for the first time? Write ✔ (yes), ✗ (no) or ? (maybe).

the visitor's clothes ☐   politics ☐
your families ☐   the weather ☐
the place you are in ☐   hobbies ☐
the visitor's journey ☐   religion ☐

Reading

7 Read these extracts from the conversation between Anna (A) and Mr Weiss (B). Which topics in Exercise 6 do they talk about?

> **1 A** … So, how was your journey?
> **B** It was fine, thanks. The plane wasn't full.
> **A** Well, not many people come to Poland at this time of year.
> **B** No, I guess not. Is it always this cold in October?
> **A** Well, not usually this cold. How was the weather in Washington?
> **B** Actually, it was quite warm. About 20 degrees.
>
> **2 B** … Where in Poland are you from?
> **A** From Krakow, in the south. Have you been there?
> **B** Yes, I have. It's a beautiful city.
> **A** What about you? Do you live in Washington?
> **B** Yes, I do, but I was born in Chicago.
>
> **3 B** … That's an amazing building – what is it?
> **A** It's the new football stadium. Are you interested in football?
> **B** I don't know much about it, but my brother loves it.
> **A** Your brother? Do you have a big family?
> **B** No, just one brother. What about you? Do you have any brothers or sisters?
> **A** Yes, I have three sisters.

8 <u>Underline</u> the questions the speakers use to introduce the topic.

Speaking

9 Work in pairs. Imagine you come from different countries. Role play a similar conversation. Take turns to be the host and the visitor. Try to keep conversation going using the questions you underlined in Exercise 8.

▶ **Get real**

Talk to someone you know who has had to spend time with overseas visitors, perhaps as part of their work. Find out what topics they talked about with these visitors, and why.

5 Who wants to be an entrepreneur?

Before you start

1 What is an *entrepreneur*? Do you know any famous entrepreneurs? Would you like to be one? Why/Why not?

Reading

2 Read the article about an American entrepreneur. Find three things that make him special.

A young entrepreneur

Jayson Meyer was sixteen when he and his younger brother Matthew started their technology company. Jayson lives in Daytona Beach, Florida, in the USA. He looks like any typical university student, but Jayson doesn't go to university. He doesn't need to. He is already a successful businessman. Jayson is co-founder and CEO (Chief Executive Officer) of Meyer Technologies, Inc.

At high school, Jayson spent a lot of time working on computers for the school and local businesses. He didn't have time for school work, but he could fix almost any computer problem. So, when he was fifteen, Jayson left school and went into business full time. With his brother, he set up a shop at the local weekend market.

The business was successful and quickly went from making $4,000 in the first year to $100,000 per year. Soon, Meyer Technologies, Inc. expanded and was making over $500,000. The company builds special computers and creates software programs for its clients. Many small businesses in Florida can't afford in-house computer support. They rely on service companies like Meyer Technologies to maintain their computers, and the company has plenty of customers. In 2000, the sales grew to over $1 million. Not bad for a business whose CEO was not old enough to vote!

Currently, Jayson is helping to grow another company called WorkSmart MD, which makes special software for doctors' offices. Jayson now employs a number of technical staff and most of them are older than their boss. Jayson himself works 80 to 100 hours a week and often sleeps at the office. He doesn't have a lot of free time to do the things that most young people do, but he doesn't mind. He says, 'I'd rather be building an international business. I think about my business most of the time – it's in my blood.'

Vocabulary

3 Find the verbs (1–8) in the article. Match them with the word or phrase (a–h) that has a similar meaning.

1	fix	a	repair
2	set up	b	depend on
3	build	c	make
4	create	d	construct
5	afford	e	start
6	rely on	f	pay for
7	maintain	g	give work to
8	employ	h	look after

4 CEO is an abbreviation for Chief Executive Officer. Use the Glossary or a dictionary to find out what these abbreviations stand for.

1 MD 2 VP 3 Inc. 4 Ltd. 5 plc

Speaking

5 Work in pairs. Role play an interview with Jayson Meyer. When you finish, change roles.

Interviewer You are a journalist from a web magazine. Your job is to interview Jayson Meyer. Here are your notes for some questions to ask. Add two more questions.

1 Do you think you are a typical seventeen year old? Why?/Why not?
2 Why did you start Meyer Technologies?
3 Who are your clients?
4 How successful is Meyer Technologies?
5
6

Jayson You are Jayson Meyer. Answer the journalist's questions. Use the information in the article in Exercise 2.

6 Would you like to do what Jason Meyer does? Why/Why not?

 ### Get real

Find out more information about other young people who are successful in business. Use the Internet or look in business magazines. Create a class display of 'teenage entrepreneurs.'

6 Writing a CV

Before you start

1 List three things you need to include in a CV.

Reading

2 Read the sections of a CV (a–h) and match them with the headings (1–8).

1 Personal statement ☐   5 Interests ☐
2 Personal details ☐   6 Other information ☐
3 Work experience ☐   7 Referees ☐
4 Languages ☐   8 Education and qualifications ☐

a Czech (mother tongue), English (fluent), Spanish (good)

b Theo Johnson, Head of Postgraduate Studies, London Business School
Sarah Lewis, Marketing Director, International Enterprises

c 1998–99 London Business School – Postgraduate Diploma in International Marketing
1994–98 University of Economics, Prague – graduated in Business Studies

d I am a hard-working and enthusiastic sales and marketing graduate, who is looking for a challenging position with an international company.

e Travel, swimming, running, reading, cinema, classical music

f
Name	Frantisek Svoboda
Address	220 Belsize Gardens, London SW2 2RT
Telephone	070 2268 2331
E-mail	fransvob@yahoo.com
Nationality	Czech
Date of birth	17th April 1976

g I spent a year travelling in the United States and Latin America between my postgraduate studies and my current job. I also worked for two summers at a summer camp for children in the US. I ran the London Marathon in 2000 and 2001.

h 2000 – date Marketing executive, JB Market Consulting, London
1999 – 2000 Marketing trainee, International Enterprises, London

Vocabulary

3 Complete (1–5) with the highlighted words.

1 Courses or exams lead to _____.
2 _____ is what you have done in your life or work.
3 A _____ is a person who has passed a university course.
4 A _____ is a person learning a job.
5 _____ is interested and excited.

Speaking

4 Work in pairs. Look at these 'rules' for writing a CV. Which ones do you agree with? Why?

- Make sure your CV is well-organized.
- Include a lot of detail – a good CV is long.
- List your education and work experience in reverse order – start with your most recent job.
- Include additional information that you think could help your application, e.g. travel experience or voluntary work.
- Don't send a covering letter – no one reads it.

5 Work in pairs. Look at the job advertisement. Discuss what qualifications and experience applicants need for this job. Do you think Frantisek Svoboda has the right qualifications and experience to apply for the job?

INTERNATIONAL MARKETING MANAGER

Lopez Garcia is a Spanish-owned investment company currently looking for a marketing professional to join our London office. The successful applicant will be responsible for:

- marketing our services to clients in the UK
- helping to develop the company's marketing plan
- travelling to Spain and Mexico for meetings with clients
- managing a team of ten people.

You need to have a marketing qualification and at least three years' experience. You must be enthusiastic, hard-working and flexible. Ability to speak Spanish is essential.

Apply in writing, with CV, to:

Jaime Aranda, Human Resources Manager, jha@st.romero.es

Writing

6 Write your CV for a job of your choice (say what it is). Use your own details and add qualifications and work experience which you hope to get in the future. Decide on the best order of the sections in Exercise 2.

▶ *Get real*
Work in pairs. Find some adverts for jobs like the one in Exercise 5. Look in newspapers or on the Internet. Choose an advert for a job you would like to do. Give your advert and CV to your partner and take theirs. Suggest ways your partner could adapt their CV to fit the job advert.

7 How bicycles can change lives

Before you start

1 Work in pairs and discuss the questions.

1 Do you have a bicycle? If so, when do you use it? If not, how would a bicycle change your life?
2 Do you know what a charity is?

Reading

2 Read this interview with David Schweidenback, who started *Pedals for Progress*. Find out:

- what Pedals for Progress does
- how Pedals for Progress works.

Pedals for Progress

a After university, I worked in a small town in Ecuador. One man in the town had a bicycle. He was richer than everyone else, because they had to walk. If you have a bicycle, you can travel much further to find employment. I realized that bicycles could make a difference to the local economy. So I decided to send used bicycles to people in developing countries.

b We collect used bicycles from local groups in the USA, where there's no market for them. We ask people to give us their old bicycle and ten dollars. We repair the bicycles, and we send a container of bicycles and parts every six months.

c We sell them. We want to create a market, so we don't give them away for free. In many countries there is a big demand but no supply, and new bicycles are very expensive. We sell our bicycles for 5% of the usual market price.

d Everyone's lives are based on the local economy. The local economy is based on the business in the town. And this is based on the movement of goods and services. If you speed up this movement, you improve the economy. Bicycles speed things up. So you get a rise in productivity, and people have more money.

e Very successful! When someone gets a bicycle from us, it means a 14% rise in income. We've done that for 62,000 people who now eat better. Take Rivas, a little town in Nicaragua, for example. It's the first place I sent bicycles to. Most people in Rivas now own one, and the local economy is doing really well.

3 Read the interview again and match the questions (1–5) with the correct paragraph (a–e).

1 Where do you get the bicycles? ☐
2 How successful is *Pedals for Progress*? ☐
3 How did you get the idea for *Pedals for Progress*? ☐
4 How do you distribute the bicycles? ☐
5 Why does sending bicycles change lives? ☐

Vocabulary

4 Match the words from the interview (1–9) with the definitions (a–i). Then write the words and phrases in your language.

1 employment ☐ _____
2 local economy ☐ _____
3 market ☐ _____
4 demand ☐ _____
5 supply ☐ _____
6 market price ☐ _____
7 goods and services ☐ _____
8 productivity ☐ _____
9 income ☐ _____

a things people buy and sell
b the business activity in a town/village
c a group of people that buys something
d the amount of money people will pay for something
e work that you get paid for
f the money you get as payment for work
g the need for something
h the amount of something you can get or buy
i the amount of work that is done

Speaking

5 Work in groups. Think of something without a market in your country, but that could help people in developing countries, e.g. old computers.

1 Imagine you are going to set up a charity like *Pedals for Progress*. Think of a name for it.
2 Discuss these questions.
   - What are you going to send?
   - How will it help people?
   - How are you going to collect it?
   - How are you going to distribute it?
3 Present your idea to the class.

▶ ### Get real

Use the Internet or magazines to find some information about unusual ideas for charities like *Pedals for Progress*. Create a class wall display with pictures and information about different charities.

8 Taking telephone messages

Before you start

1 Work in pairs and discuss the questions.

1 When you answer the phone at home, do you say:
  a 'hello'?   c the phone number?
  b your name?   d something else?

2 How do people answer the phone at work?

3 How do you say these phone numbers in English?
  a 07791 842287   b 0033 10 45469011

4 Say your own phone number in English.

Reading

2 Read these two calls and complete the notes.

1 A Hello. AGM Finance. Jana speaking. Can I help you?
  B Hello. Can I speak to Tomas Czeska, please?
  A Who's calling, please?
  B This is Anna Lee.
  A Just a moment … I'm sorry, the line is busy. Do you want to hold on, or call back later?
  B Can I leave a message?
  A Of course.
  B Can you ask him to call me on 0121 334 8798?
  A OK, 0121 334 8798.
  B That's right. Can you say I need to speak to him urgently?
  A I'll give him the message.
  B Thanks. Goodbye.

2 A Hello. Ikon Technology. Can I help you?
  B Good morning. This is Paul Danielsson from Stockholm. Can I speak to Jo Stein, please?
  A I'm sorry, she's not in the office today. Can I take a message?
  B Yes. I need to talk to her about our meeting. Can you ask her call me as soon as possible?
  A Yes, of course. Can I have your number?
  B Yes, it's 0046 8 5678 6769.
  A So that's 0046 8 5678 6769.
  B Yes, and let me give you my mobile number. It's 07990 202022.
  A OK, Mr Danielsson, I'll give her the message.
  B Thank you.
  A You're welcome. Goodbye.

1	2
Message for: _____	Message for: _____
Caller's name: _____	Caller's name: _____
Number(s): _____	Number(s): _____
Message: _____	Message: _____
_____	_____

Vocabulary

3 Look at these phrases from the two phone calls. Does the person *answering* the call (A) or the person *making* the call (B) say them? Write A or B in the boxes.

1 … speaking. Can I help you?   ☐
2 Who's calling, please?   ☐
3 This is … from …   ☐
4 Can I leave a message?   ☐
5 I'm sorry, the line is busy.   ☐
6 Can I have your number?   ☐
7 Can I speak to …, please?   ☐
8 Just a moment, please.   ☐
9 Do you want to hold on, or call back later?   ☐
10 Can you ask him to call me back?   ☐
11 Can I take a message?   ☐
12 Can you ask him …?   ☐

Speaking

4 Work in pairs. Read the phone calls in Exercise 2 aloud. Take turns to be A and B.

5 Now make two more calls using the information below. Take turns to be A and B.

1 A Call Ikon Technology. You need to speak to Anya Markova. If she's not there, leave a message. Use your own name and telephone number.
  B You work for Ikon Technology. Anya Markova's line is busy at the moment. Offer to take a message. Take the caller's name and phone number.

2 A Call your friend Chris in America. If he/she's not there, leave a message asking him/her to call you. Use your own name and telephone number.
  B You live in America. You are Chris's brother/sister. Chris is out at the moment. Offer to take a message. Take the caller's name and phone number.

Writing

6 Write one of the calls you made in Exercise 5. Use the calls in Exercise 2 to help you.

▶ ### Get real
Work in pairs. Write some instructions for a phone call on a piece of paper. Write instructions for A and B, as in Exercise 5. Then give your instructions to another pair. A makes the call and leaves a message; B answers the call and takes the messsage. Listen and check that the information is all correct.

9 Writing a business e-mail

Before you start

1 Why do people use e-mail in business? Make a list of reasons.

Reading

2 Read some 'rules' (on the right) for writing good business e-mails. Which rules do you follow?

3 Read the e-mail below from a student to a company about their work experience programme. Which rules in Exercise 2 does he break?

Vocabulary

4 Look at the phrases in *italics* (1–6) in the e-mail. Match them with the formal phrases (a–f) below.

a Could you send me more information … ☐

b I look forward to hearing from you. ☐

c I am writing to ask about … ☐

d My name is Luigi Ferrara … ☐

e Dear Ms Lewis ☐

f I am interested in applying for … ☐

5 Here are some phrases to use in e-mails. Write starting (S), ending (E), saying why you are writing (W) or requesting (R) after each one and the ones in Exercise 4.

1 My name is …

2 I'm a student at … (school / college)

3 Dear Amanda (informal)

4 Thank you for your message.

5 With best wishes.

6 Please e-mail me if you need more information.

7 Yours sincerely

8 Thank you for your e-mail of 20th August.

9 Please send me details of …

Writing

6 Work in pairs. Rewrite the e-mail on the right using the rules in Exercise 2 and some of the phrases in Exercise 5.

▶ Get real

You are interested in taking part in a work experience programme for business students. Write an e-mail to a company that offers such programmes. Organize your e-mail like this:

- introduce yourself
- explain why you are writing to them
- request some information about the programme.

Don't forget to start and end the e-mail in an appropriate way.

How to write an effective e-mail

1 Use a subject line that tells the other person what the e-mail is about. Don't just write *Information* or *Your e-mail.*

2 If you are writing to someone you don't know, start by saying who you are and why you are writing.

3 Use written greetings *(Dear Mr Smith)* and endings *(Yours sincerely)*, just as you would in a letter.

4 Use short, clear sentences.

5 Use paragraphs for different subjects. Leave a space between paragraphs.

6 In business e-mails, always use a formal and polite tone. Don't be too informal or familiar.

7 Don't use emoticons, e.g. ☺, or acronyms, e.g. BTW *(by the way).*

8 Don't write in CAPITAL LETTERS – this is like shouting.

9 Don't repeat yourself – try not to use the same word more than once in a paragraph.

10 Check your spelling and punctuation – are they correct? If you are worried about your spelling, use a spell check.

To: Amanda Lewis, Human Resources Manager

From: Luigi Ferrara

Subject: Information

¹ *Hello Amanda!*

² *I'm Luigi* from Pescara. ³ *Can you tell me about* your student programme? I know your company takes students who want some work experience in their holidays, and ⁴ *I want to apply for* the programme because I want to get some experience of working in a big multinational company and I also want to practise my English and make it better, because I think it is VERY BAD. Sorry about that!! I want to know more about the program, so ⁵ *please give me some more information*, in particular the dates, the details of the daily work, how much you pay, where I can stay, etc. I study marketing so I would like to work in the marketing department if it is possible. BTW, I'm a 20-year-old student of business living in Italy. Sorry, I forgot to tell you that ☺.

⁶ *Send me your reply soon.* Thanks a lot. Bye.
Luigi

10 Getting started in business

Before you start

1 How much free time do you have outside school? How do you spend it? Would you like to spend some of your free time earning money?

Reading

2 This article gives advice for someone who wants to start their own business. Match the questions (a–f) with the paragraphs (1–6).

a How much will my business cost to run? ☐
b How do I get started? ☐
c Where will I get the money? ☐
d Can I make a profit? ☐
e How much money will I make? ☐
f How much should I charge? ☐

What do Juan from Spain and Jessica from the USA have in common? They are both teenagers running successful businesses. Juan, 16, has a gardening business with 75 clients and three employees. Jessica's company cleans new houses. She started it when she was 14. If you want to start a business, good planning is important. Here are some tips.

1 Get organized. Decide what your skills are. Find out if there is a market for them in your area, e.g. ask your neighbours what they need. Babysitting, coaching for exams or sports, and computer training are all possibilities.

2 Decide how much money you need to start your business. Think about how to get the **capital**. You can use your own money or you can ask the bank for a **loan**. If you get a loan, be sure you can afford to pay the **interest**.

3 Calculate your **costs**. First, work out your fixed costs, for example, the rent on your office or the interest on a loan. Then add your variable costs, for example, equipment or tax (if you pay it).

4 Work out how much to charge for your service. Find out what other people are charging and use this to set your own prices.

5 Your **revenue** is the amount of money you receive from selling your service. You need to calculate this very carefully. Your revenue is the number of hours worked multiplied by (x) the price per hour.

6 Your business will make a **profit** if your revenue for a year is more than your costs. If your costs are higher than the revenue, you'll make a **loss**. Work out carefully the number of hours you need to work.

Vocabulary

3 Match the **highlighted** words in the text with the definitions (1–7). Write them in your language.

1 an amount of money you need to start a business _____ _____
2 the money you receive from selling a product or service _____ _____
3 what you make if your revenue is more than your costs _____ _____
4 what you make if your revenue is less than your costs _____ _____
5 an amount of money that someone, e.g. the bank, lends you _____ _____
6 money you pay for things and services to run your business _____ _____
7 an amount you pay for borrowing money, e.g. from the bank _____ _____

Speaking

4 Work in pairs. Look at this summary of two companies' profit and loss accounts for next year. For each company, calculate:

1 Pre-tax profit (= revenue minus costs)
2 Profit after tax (= pre-tax profit minus tax).

Which company will be more profitable?

	Company A (€s)	Company B (€s)
Revenue	17,575	18,850
Costs	14,940	16,625
Pre-tax profit	_____	_____
Tax	790	670
Profit after tax	_____	_____

5 Work in pairs or small groups. You have decided to start a small business to earn extra money outside school. Discuss these questions.

• What service are you going to sell?
• How much capital do you need to start it?
• What are your fixed and variable costs?
• What price will you charge?
• How many hours' work will cover your costs?
• How much profit will you make?

6 Write a profit and loss account to show your plan. Use the table in Exercise 4 to help you. Present your plan to the class.

> ## Get real
> Talk to someone who has their own business. Find out how they started it. Was it easy or difficult? Is their company profitable?

11 Doing business in Japan

Before you start

1 Work in pairs and discuss the questions.

1 What do you think it's important to know about another country if you are going on holiday or if you are going to work or study there?

2 What do you know about Japan?

Reading

2 Read this information for visitors to Japan. Is it for tourists, business people or students?

a When you meet someone in Japan, it is normal to bow. However, it's OK to shake hands, particularly with people who work in international companies. It's not a good idea to hug people.

b Always use chopsticks with your right hand. Place them on the side of a dish after you have started eating, not on the table. And never leave them standing in the rice bowl – it's bad luck.

c Your business card should state your name, company and position in your language and (on the back) in Japanese. Always give and receive cards with both hands. Treat other people's cards with respect – look at them carefully before putting them away. Never write or make notes on them.

d Send an agenda in advance and make it clear what the meeting is about. Also, send any documents – translated into Japanese. Try to find out who will attend, and check if your hosts speak English. If not, you will need an interpreter.

e Allow time for proper introductions and small talk as a friendly atmosphere is helpful. If there is silence during the meeting, don't worry – this is thinking time. Always take notes, and write to thank your hosts and confirm any decisions.

f You shouldn't use someone's first name until you have met several times and know each other well. Be sure to use titles such as *Mr*, *Ms*, or *-san*, but never use *-san* when referring to yourself.

g Japanese businessmen wear a blue or grey suit, a white or blue shirt and dark tie. Businesswomen should also wear a suit and use only a little jewellery and make-up. In summer when it's hot and humid, it's a good idea to pack several changes of clothes.

3 Read the text again. Match the headings (1–7) with the paragraphs (a–g).

1 What to wear ☐
2 Business cards ☐
3 Eating out ☐
4 Greetings ☐
5 During and after meetings ☐
6 Talking to others ☐
7 Before a meeting ☐

4 Here are some *do*s and *don't*s about working in Japan. There are several more in the article. Find another two of each and add them to the lists.

*Do*s …
bow when you meet someone
use chopsticks with your right hand

_____

_____

*Don't*s …
hug people when you meet them
put chopsticks on the table

_____

_____

Vocabulary

5 Use these phrases to make sentences with the information you found in Exercise 4.

*Do*s	*Don't*s
You should …	*You shouldn't …*
Always …	*Never …*
It's OK to …	*It's not OK to …*
It's a good idea to …	*It's not a good idea to …*
It's important to …	*It's important not to …*
It's polite to …	*It's not polite to …*

Speaking

6 Work in pairs. Make a list of *do*s and *don't*s for visitors to your country.

Writing

7 Use your list to write some information like the article in Exercise 2.

▶ ## Get real

Choose another country with a business culture that is very different from your country, e.g. China, South Korea, Brazil, Saudi Arabia. Use newspapers, magazines, books or the Internet to find information about doing business in this country. Make a list of *do*s and *don't*s for that country. Create a class file on 'Business Culture.'

Before you start

1 Work in pairs. Have you ever taken part in a discussion with a large group of people?

1 If you have, how did you feel when you had to speak, e.g. nervous, confident?

2 If you have not, would you like to? Why/Why not?

Reading

2 Here are some 'rules' of things to do before a meeting. Read the rules and the e-mail below. Tick (✔) the rules that the e-mail follows.

1 Send an agenda several days before. ☐

2 Make sure everyone knows the time and date of the meeting. ☐

3 Say where it will be, and how to get there. ☐

4 Make it clear why you are having the meeting. ☐

5 Make sure everyone knows who will be there. ☐

6 Appoint a chairperson and note taker. ☐

7 If necessary, ask people to prepare to talk about a particular point. ☐

8 Make sure people know what will happen next. ☐

Memo

To: Project team
From: Paul Heaton
Date: 24th June
Subject: Meeting

Dear all

This e-mail is to remind you about the meeting at 10.00 on Friday, 28th June. The purpose of the meeting is to discuss the next stage of the Randall project.

I attach an agenda with the main points for discussion. If you have any other points you want to discuss, please let me know. I also attach a list of participants, so you know who will be at the meeting.

The chairperson will be Suzanna Novotna. We need someone to take the minutes so there is a record of what we talked about. Michael, can you do this, please? You will receive the minutes as soon as possible after the meeting, together with a list of action points and responsibilities.

I look forward to seeing you all.

With best wishes

Paul

Vocabulary

3 Match the words and phrases from the e-mail (1–7) with the definitions (a–g). Then write the words and phrases in your language.

1 purpose ☐ _____
2 agenda ☐ _____
3 main points ☐ _____
4 participants ☐ _____
5 chairperson ☐ _____
6 minutes ☐ _____
7 action points ☐ _____

a notes of what is said at a meeting

b the people who take part in a meeting

c a list of what will happen at a meeting

d the things to do after a meeting

e the person who keeps control of a meeting

f the reason for or aim of having a meeting

g the most important things to talk about

Speaking

4 Work in pairs. Here are some tips for speaking in meetings. Which ones do you agree with?

- Only speak if you have something important to say.
- Let people finish their point before you speak – never interrupt.
- On your turn, speak for as long as possible.
- It's OK to interrupt someone.
- It's OK to make grammatical mistakes, as long as people understand you.

5 Work in groups. You have decided to hold a meeting to plan social events for next term.

- When and where will the meeting be?
- Who will be the participants?
- What are the main points?
- Who will be the chairperson?
- Who will take the minutes?
- Who will speak about particular points?
- What will happen after the meeting?

Writing

6 Write an e-mail to tell the class about the meeting. Include information about all the points you discussed in Exercise 5.

▶ **Get real**

Talk to someone you know who attends business meetings. Find out how they prepare for the meeting and what happens during the meeting. Tell the class.

13 Taking part in a meeting

Before you start

1 Look at some things that people say about speaking in meetings. Tick the ones you agree with then compare your answers with a partner.

1 It's difficult to think of the right words. ☐
2 I always have a lot to say. ☐
3 I don't like it when people disagree with me. ☐
4 People are always interrupting me. ☐
5 I'm not sure if people always understand me. ☐

Reading

2 Look at this agenda and answer the questions.

1 What is the meeting about?
2 How many people will attend the meeting?
3 What is Carla's role?

AGENDA

Meeting Friday 28th June

Chairperson: Clare

Participants: Ella, Tom, Jake, Mila, Frank

Minutes: Carla

Purpose of meeting: To plan the visit by exchange students 16th–20th September

Main points:

1 Daily activities   3 Accommodation
2 Evening activities   4 End-of-week celebration

3 Now read part of the meeting and answer the questions. (Clare = A, Jake = B, Ella = C, Tom = D)

1 What do the speakers agree about?
2 What do Tom and Ella disagree about?

A ... So, now we need to talk about point 4, the end-of-week celebration. Can we brainstorm some ideas? Jake, what do you think?
B Why don't we have a party?
C Yes, I agree. Definitely a party.
A OK, that's a good idea. Any ideas for what kind of party? What about you, Tom?
D What about having a big party for all the students and their families? We could use the main hall, so people can dance. We could get a band ...
C Yes, that's right. We want somewhere to dance, but I don't think we should have a band. I think we should have a DJ.
D Well, I don't agree with you. In my opinion, a band is much more exciting than a DJ.
C Yes, but a DJ can play different types of music ...
A OK, Ella, we can decide later. Let's agree that we're going to have music.
B Excuse me, can I say something?
A Of course.
B My brother is a DJ ...

Vocabulary

4 Look at the headings. Find two phrases in the dialogue which do each of these things and write them under the headings.

ask for ideas / opinions

1 _____ 2 _____

make a suggestion

1 _____ 2 _____

give your opinion

1 _____ 2 _____

agree

1 _____ 2 _____

disagree

1 _____ 2 _____

interrupt

1 _____ 2 _____

Speaking

5 Work in groups of four. Read the dialogue aloud. Take turns to be Clare, Ella, Tom and Jake.

6 Work in different groups to have a meeting.

Your class teacher is leaving the school. A few of you are having a meeting to decide what to buy him/her and when to present it. Appoint a chairperson and someone to take minutes. Use phrases from the table in Exercise 4 to:

1 ask for ideas/opinions
2 make suggestions
3 give your opinion
4 agree or disagree
5 interrupt.

Writing

7 Write an e-mail to the rest of the class to tell them what you decided in your meeting and to invite them to the presentation. Use these phrases.

As you know, X is leaving on …
We have decided to …
We would like you to join us …
Can you please …

▶ ## Get real

When are you next going to plan an activity as a class, e.g. a class trip, an end-of-year party? When you plan it, hold a class meeting to decide what to do, like the ones in this unit.

Before you start

1 Do you have a mobile phone? Do you use it a lot? Who pays for the calls?

Reading

2 Why do you have a mobile phone? Read these quotes. Which reason is closest to yours?

1 I have it in case I get into trouble, or if I need to contact someone quickly.
2 I spend a lot of time on the phone at home. It's better and cheaper for my parents if I have a mobile, because I have to pay for my calls.
3 I like to be able to text or chat to my friends, any time I want.
4 Everyone has one – if you don't have a mobile it's bad for your social life.

3 Look at the charts and answer the questions.

1 Match these labels with the charts.
a pie chart ☐ a graph ☐ a bar chart ☐

2 Which chart is best for showing:
trends? ☐ proportions and percentages? ☐
comparisons? ☐

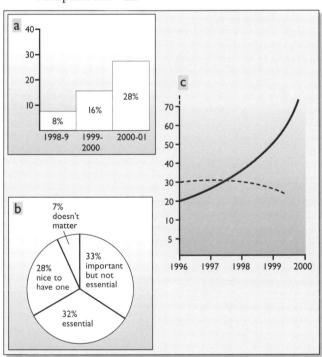

4 Read the texts and match them with the charts.

> **1** A mobile phone is stolen in the UK every three minutes. Almost half of the victims (48%) of mobile phone theft are under 18. The average age of the thief is 16. In 2000–01, 28% of all robberies involved a mobile phone, compared with 16% in 1999–2000. This was double the number for 1998–99, when only 8% involved a mobile.

> **2** Smoking among 15 year olds fell from 30% to 23% between 1996 and 1999, while mobile phone ownership among 15 to 17 year olds rose from low levels in 1996 to 70% by August 2000. Is there a link? Experts think that using a mobile satisfies the same teenage needs as smoking. Both are a way of taking part in the social life of the group. Both offer a sense of style and individuality, making the user feel adult and independent. And many teenagers can't afford to do both.

> **3** According to research, the majority of 18 to 24 year olds (88%) currently have a mobile phone for personal use. In a recent survey of their views, 32% said they can't live without their mobile phone. One in three (33%) said a mobile is important, but not essential and 28% said it's nice to have a mobile, but they could live without it. Only 7% said it doesn't matter whether they have one or not.

Vocabulary

5 Find and <u>underline</u> the words and phrases (1–6) on the left in the texts. Then match them with the words and phrases (a–f) with a similar meaning.

1 the majority of	a went up
2 one in three	b most
3 fell	c 48%
4 rose	d twice
5 almost half	e a third
6 double	f went down

Speaking

6 Work in pairs. You are going to conduct a survey of people in your class (or another class).

1 Choose a or b. Find out about:
   a people's attitudes to something, e.g. smoking, the Internet, texting
   b the number of people who have taken up a particular activity now which they didn't do two years ago, e.g. using the Internet.

2 Prepare some questions to ask.

3 Interview at least ten people.

4 Choose the best chart to show the results of your survey. Draw your chart and present it to the class. Create a class display.

▶ **Get real**
Take the other option from Exercise 6 (the one you didn't do) and ask a few people outside your school, e.g. in your family. Put the results in a chart and present them to the class.

15 Making arrangements by telephone

Before you start

1 Work in pairs and discuss the questions.

1 Say these dates in English:
   - a 10/09/02
   - b 24/03/03
   - c 01/11/99
   - d 14/07/87

2 Say these times in English. Say each time in two ways.
   - a 10.30
   - b 3.45
   - c 10.20
   - d 11.05

3 Which expressions do we use with *in, at* or *on*?
   - a _____ the weekend
   - b _____ Wednesday
   - c _____ the summer
   - d _____ the afternoon
   - e _____ 12.30

Reading

2 Two people are arranging a meeting. Read the phone call and complete Elana's meeting planner. (A = Michael, B = Elana)

> A Hello, Michael Kennedy.
> B Hello, Michael. It's Elana …
> A Hello, Elana, how are you?
> B I'm fine, thank you. And you?
> A Very well, thanks. What can I do for you?
> B I'd like to arrange a meeting with you.
> A OK, no problem …
> B It's about the plans for the new employees' training week.
> A Fine. When shall we meet?
> B One day next week?
> A OK. How about Tuesday in the afternoon? That's the 15th.
> B No, I'm afraid I'm busy all day on Tuesday. What about Thursday or Friday?
> A Sorry, I can't make Friday. I'm on a course. But Thursday is fine. Morning or afternoon?
> B The afternoon is best for me.
> A OK. Shall we say 2.30?
> B Yes, that's fine. Where shall we meet?
> A You've got a bigger office!
> B OK. So that's half past two on Thursday 17th August, in my office.
> A Right.
> B Thanks, Michael. I'll look forward to seeing you then.

Meeting with:	
Date:	
Time:	
Place:	
Reason for meeting:	

3 Read the call again. Find and <u>underline</u> one or more phrases which:

1 say you want a meeting
2 explain the reason for the meeting
3 suggest a day or time
4 agree to a day or time
5 say no and give a reason
6 ask about the place
7 confirm the details.

Speaking

4 Work in pairs. Read the phone call in Exercise 2 aloud. Take turns to be A and B.

5 Work in different pairs. Practise making arrangements on the phone. Use the diagram to help you. Take turns to be A and B. Start and end the conversation like the one in Exercise 2.

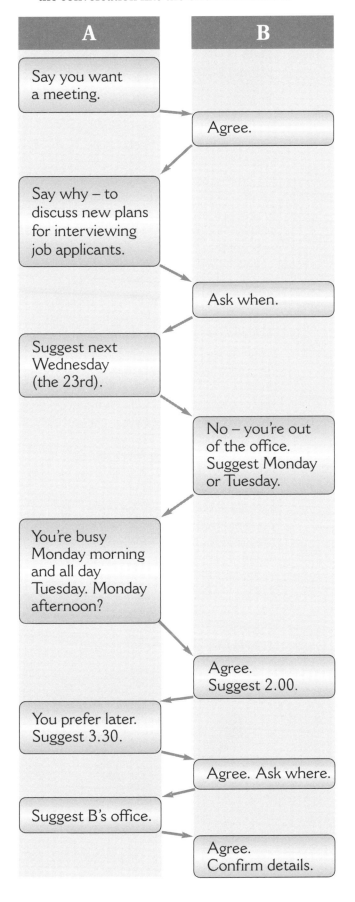

A	B
Say you want a meeting.	
	Agree.
Say why – to discuss new plans for interviewing job applicants.	
	Ask when.
Suggest next Wednesday (the 23rd).	
	No – you're out of the office. Suggest Monday or Tuesday.
You're busy Monday morning and all day Tuesday. Monday afternoon?	
	Agree. Suggest 2.00.
You prefer later. Suggest 3.30.	
	Agree. Ask where.
Suggest B's office.	
	Agree. Confirm details.

6 Work on your own. This is your business diary page for next week. Write down at least four appointments on different days. Write the time and place.

17 Monday

18 Tuesday

19 Wednesday

20 Thursday

21 Friday

22 Saturday

23 Sunday

7 Work in groups of four. You need to arrange a meeting at a time when you are all free. Decide the reason for the meeting and agree when and where it will take place.

Writing

8 Look back at the phone call in Exercise 2. Write a short e-mail from Elana to Michael to confirm the arrangement. Use these phrases:

Thank you for agreeing to a meeting to discuss ...
This is to confirm the time and date of our meeting ...
We will meet in ... at ... on ...
I look forward to seeing you.

9 Now write another e-mail confirming the arrangements you made in Exercise 5.

▶ **Get real**
Think about how people make arrangements on the telephone in your language. Are there any differences in the way you do it and in English? If so, what are they?

16 | Teenage inventions

Before you start

1 Do you know anyone who is deaf, i.e. who can't hear? How do they communicate? Do you know any sign language?

Reading

2 Read the information about two inventions by teenagers and complete the chart.

	Invention A	Invention B
1 What is the invention?		
2 What problem does it solve?		
3 How does it work?		

A

Home Business Culture Politics

When eighteen-year-old Ryan Patterson read a story in his local newspaper about a teenage girl who couldn't hear or speak, it gave him an idea. The girl used sign language, but she needed a human translator with her all the time.

Ryan has designed a glove that can translate sign language into text. It uses electronic sensors to read the hand movements of the person who is wearing it. Then it transmits the data to a portable device that displays the text on screen. The device only translates the alphabet, but a special program allows the user to adapt hand movements. The user can give special meanings to certain hand movements.

Ryan has built two prototypes using a leather golf glove. He has tested it with students from the National Technical Institute for the Deaf (NTID). He has a patent on the device, which means that he owns the idea. He's now thinking about starting his own company so he can develop the design and market it.

B

Home Business Culture Politics

Hanna & Heather Craig

Hanna and Heather Craig, twin sisters aged seventeen from Alaska, have invented a new winter rescue device: a 1.2 metre-long robot called the Ice Crawler. The robot is designed to take a rope to a person in a dangerous situation, for example, on thin ice or very soft snow.

The Ice Crawler's body consists of two tracks made of silicon-reinforced rubber, which is very strong and flexible even at extremely cold temperatures. This means the robot can move over ice, snow or rough ground without getting stuck. The Ice Crawler is operated by a control panel. This allows the rescue team to stay at a safe distance from the victim. The control panel enables the user to steer the robot, move it forwards and backwards, and switch the power on and off.

The robot runs on two 12-volt drive motors – one on each of the tracks. These are powered by a 12-volt battery. A plastic tube carries the control panel's wiring. It also holds the rope that pulls the victim back to safety. A video camera is attached to the front of the robot. This helps the rescue team to see where the Ice Crawler is going in snowy conditions or on very rough ground.

Ice Crawler

Vocabulary (Text A)

3 Find and underline a word in Text A that means:

1 a person who changes something from one language to another (noun) _____

2 something that can detect, heat, light, movement, etc. (noun) _____

3 send information electronically (verb) _____

4 a piece of equipment made for a special purpose (noun) _____

5 to make or change something for a special purpose (verb) _____

6 the first model or design of something (noun) _____

7 the official right to make and sell a product (noun) _____

4 Now write the words in your language.

5 Here are some stages in the process of inventing a new product. Number them in a logical order.

a build a prototype ☐

b patent the device ☐

c have an idea ☐

d test the prototype ☐

e design the product ☐

f talk to a company about building it ☐

g build a better prototype ☐

Vocabulary (Text B)

6 Look at Text B again. Label the diagram of the Ice Crawler with words from the text.

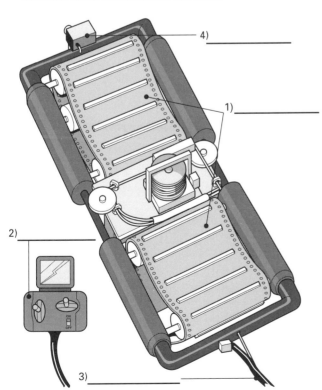

4) _____

1) _____

2) _____

3) _____

7 Complete this paragraph about another robot using the words in the box.

> allows ■ attached to ■ consists of ■
> enables ■ designed to ■ operated by
> ■ powered by ■ runs on

The Trackster is ¹_____ find people trapped in damaged buildings after an earthquake or an explosion. It ²_____ the rescue team to search for victims from a safe distance. The Trackster ³_____ a small body with four tracks. It is ⁴_____ a hand-held control panel. This sends a radio signal to the robot. The Trackster ⁵_____ an electric motor which is ⁶_____ a ten-volt portable battery. A video camera is ⁷_____ the front of the robot – this ⁸_____ the rescue team to see if there is anyone in the building.

Speaking

8 Work in pairs. What do you think of the inventions in Exercise 2? Could you invent something similar?

1 Brainstorm an idea for an invention that might help someone with a disability, e.g. someone who can't see or who can't walk, or perhaps an old person who can't move around much.

2 Design your invention then draw a diagram of it.

3 Explain your invention to the class. Say:
   • what the invention is
   • what problem it solves
   • how it works.

▶ Get real

Search the Internet or magazines for other unusual inventions. If you find something interesting, bring it to the class. Explain it to some other students.

Before you start

1 Work in pairs. Make a list of things that are important when choosing a job, e.g. earning a lot of money, working for a big company, helping other people. You have one minute.

2 Why do people choose these jobs?

a teacher b banker c doctor d engineer

Reading

3 Read about the quotes from two people talking about their jobs. Which one is motivated by:

1 helping other people? _____

2 earning a lot of money? _____

Marie, accountant

I work in the finance department of a large company. There are a lot of benefits. For example, if the company makes a profit, all the employees get a bonus. There's also a profit share, but that's only for managers. I have a company car and I also travel abroad quite a lot – always business class and on expenses, of course. We also get a pension and private health insurance. The company pays for its staff to go on training courses to develop their professional skills. And we get free membership of the local gym. There are also rewards: it's hard work, but I get a lot of satisfaction from it. People recognize it if you do a good job, so there are good prospects for promotion.

Tom, physiotherapist

I work for the health service. There are a lot of rewards: the main one is the job satisfaction. I get a real sense of achievement when someone says 'thank you.' You know you're doing a worthwhile job. If you work hard, there are opportunities for promotion. I like the responsibility of making a difference to people's lives. There are some benefits. We don't get bonuses or anything like that, but there's a very good pension. The health service pays for us to go on training courses, and people with children get help with paying for childcare. If I visit patients at home, I get a travel allowance, but it's not very much.

4 Look at this list of things that motivate people and tick the things Marie and Tom mention.

	Marie	Tom
pension	☐	☐
training	☐	☐
profit share	☐	☐
expenses	☐	☐
company car	☐	☐
business class travel	☐	☐
private health insurance	☐	☐
bonus	☐	☐
travel allowance	☐	☐
subsidized childcare	☐	☐
job satisfaction	☐	☐
promotion	☐	☐
responsibility	☐	☐
gym membership	☐	☐
doing something worthwhile	☐	☐

5 Which things in the list in Exercise 4 are benefits (extra things you get from your employer)? Which ones are rewards (things that make you feel good about the job)?

Vocabulary

6 Check the meaning of any words in Exercise 4 that you don't know in the Glossary or a dictionary. Then work in pairs to test your partner. Cover the list of words. Say the word in your language. Your partner has to say it in English.

Speaking

7 Choose five rewards or benefits from the list in Exercise 4. Number them in order of importance to you. Explain your order to another student.

Writing

8 Choose one of these jobs, or another job you know about:

flight attendant ■ dentist ■ architect ■ hotel receptionist ■ salesperson ■ nurse

1 Make a list of the rewards and benefits of the job.

2 Imagine this is your job. Write a short text describing the rewards and benefits. Use the texts in Exercise 3 to help you.

▶ **Get real**

Interview two people you know about their jobs. Find out about the benefits and rewards they get from their job. Tell the class.

Before you start

1 Think of things that you have in your home or school, e.g. a fridge, a TV, a computer. What are the names of the companies that made them?

Reading

2 Read the text and correct the statements below.

International trade is when companies from one country sell their products or services in other countries. For example, the UK produces cars, machinery, oil, and chemicals, which it exports to **overseas markets**. Other British **exports** include services like banking and travel. These earn **foreign currency** for the UK. **Imports** to the UK include cars, food, and electrical goods.

Many companies set up **subsidiaries** overseas, either for manufacturing or for distribution, or both. These companies are called **multinationals** – Shell, Ford, and Sony are examples. Most multinational companies 'think global and act local.' This means that they try to understand and cater for the needs of every market they sell in.

International trade means there are more companies competing with each other to sell their products. This means lower prices, which is good for customers because they pay less and have more choice. Producers, however, make less profit. Multinational companies often look for ways to reduce their costs, for example, by manufacturing their products in countries where **labour costs** are cheap.

Changes in the **exchange rate** can make a company more or less competitive. The exchange rate is the amount of one currency needed to buy another currency. For example, in 2002, one British pound bought about 200 Japanese yen, so the exchange rate was 1:200. If the exchange rate falls, exports become cheaper, so companies become more competitive. If the exchange rate rises, exports become more expensive, so companies become less competitive.

1 British companies don't sell overseas.
2 Multinational companies sell the same products in different markets.
3 Increased competition is good for producers and bad for customers.
4 Changes in the exchange rate are not important in international trade.

Vocabulary

3 Match the **highlighted** words and phrases in the text with the definitions (1–8). Then write the words and phrases in your language.

1 what a company pays for its workers
＿＿＿＿＿ ＿＿＿＿＿
2 the type of money used in another country or market ＿＿＿＿＿ ＿＿＿＿＿
3 the value of one currency compared to another ＿＿＿＿＿ ＿＿＿＿＿
4 smaller companies that are part of a larger company ＿＿＿＿＿ ＿＿＿＿＿
5 companies that operate in more than one country ＿＿＿＿＿ ＿＿＿＿＿
6 things produced in your country and sold in other countries ＿＿＿＿＿ ＿＿＿＿＿ .
7 places abroad where you can sell your products ＿＿＿＿＿ ＿＿＿＿＿
8 things produced in other countries and sold in your country ＿＿＿＿＿ ＿＿＿＿＿

4 Look at the word map for the verb *compete*. Make similar word maps for these words: *produce, employ, operate*. Use a dictionary to help you.

competitor — competitive — **compete** — competition — competitiveness

Speaking

5 Work in pairs. You work for a multinational company. You are looking for a new overseas market to manufacture and sell your products in. Look at this information about two possible international markets. Discuss which market seems better, A or B.

	Market A	Market B
Competition from other exporters	high	medium
Exchange rates	stable	rising
Labour costs	$$$	$
Personal income of the population	$$$$$	$$

> ### Get real
> Use newspapers, magazine articles or the Internet to find out about a multinational company that interests you. Find out what it makes, what are its main markets, and where its subsidiaries are. Prepare a short talk.

Before you start

1 What is a report? Why do people write reports? Who reads them?

2 Work in pairs. Discuss these questions.

1 How many hours a day do you spend watching TV?
   a less than 1 hour   **c** 2–3 hours
   b 1–2 hours   **d** more than 3 hours

2 Do you watch more or less TV at weekends?

3 What kind of programmes do you watch?

> cartoons ■ dramas/films ■ soaps ■ sport
> ■ news ■ documentaries ■ music shows,
> e.g. on MTV ■ comedies ■ chat shows
> ■ games and quizzes

Reading

3 Look at the extracts (1-5) from a report. Who would be particularly interested in this report?

1 students
2 advertising companies
3 psychiatrists

4 Match the extracts (1–5) with the headings (a–e).

a Conclusion ☐
b Findings ☐
c Introduction ☐
d Procedure ☐
e Method ☐

---

1 **Report on research project into the TV-watching habits of school students.**

The purpose of this research was to find out how many hours of TV students watch in a typical week. It also aimed to find out what kind of programmes they watch. In addition, it looked at the kind of programmes watched by male and female students to find out if there was any difference in their preferences.

2 We carried out the research by interviewing students in the target group – school students aged 14–18, both male and female. We spoke to students from a number of different schools in five different cities. We interviewed 120 students in total, 60 boys and 60 girls.

3 We asked all the interviewees the same questions. First, we asked them if they have a TV in their bedroom as well as the main TV in the house; then if they usually watch TV alone or with their family. Next, we asked what kind of TV programmes they like and how many hours of TV they watch in a typical week. After that, we asked how many hours they spend watching TV on school days (Monday to Friday) and how many hours at the weekend. Finally, we asked how many hours they spend watching the different kinds of programmes.

4 We found that 60% of interviewees have a TV in their bedroom and most watch it alone. On school days, 40% of boys and 50% of girls watch TV for two hours or more, mostly between 6.00 and 9.00 p.m. Only 20% of boys and 15% of girls watch less than one hour. However, at weekends, 60% of boys and 70% of girls watch more than two hours a day, in the mornings and in the evenings.
Boys prefer to watch sport, cartoons and music programmes, whereas girls prefer to watch soaps, dramas and music. Only 18% of boys and 16% of girls say they watch news regularly. However, more girls than boys watch documentaries.

5 Our research shows that the best time for TV advertisements aimed at young people in this age group is between 6.00 and 9.00 p.m. on weekdays, and in the mornings. In addition, advertisers whose target market is mainly girls should aim to place their ads between soaps, dramas, and music programmes. If the target market is boys, they should place ads between sport, cartoons, and music programmes.

Vocabulary

5 Look at Extract 3 again. Complete this paragraph with the words in the box. Use capital letters where necessary.

> after that ∎ first ∎ finally ∎ then ∎ next

¹_____, we asked the interviewees if they own a mobile phone; ²_____ what make of phone they own. ³_____, we asked what they use it for – emergencies, chatting to friends, etc. ⁴_____, we asked how many hours they spend on the phone each week. ⁵_____, we asked them who pays for the calls.

6 Look at Extracts 1 and 4.

1 Find and underline:
   a a word and a phrase used to add information
   b two words used to connect two facts that are different.

2 Complete this paragraph with the words and phrases you have underlined. You have to use one word twice.

> The purpose of this research was to find out what students aged 14–18 use their mobile phones for. It **a**_____ aimed to find out what kind of phones they use. **b**_____, it asked how many hours they spend on the phone, and **c**_____ if there is any difference between boys and girls in how they use their phones.
>
> We found that girls prefer to use their phones to chat with friends, **d**_____ boys prefer to send text messages. **e**_____, more girls than boys keep in touch with their parents by texting.

Speaking

7 Look at Extract 3 again. Write the questions that the interviewers asked. Work in pairs and interview your partner.

8 Prepare a short survey about one of the following options. Think about the questions you will ask. Then interview as many people as possible in your class or school.

a Music

Find out the following information:
- how many people have music in their bedroom, or a personal stereo
- where they listen to music
- how many hours they spend listening to music on weekdays
- how many hours they spend listening to music at weekends
- what kinds of music they listen to.

b Exercise

Find out the following information:
- how many people exercise regularly
- what type(s) of exercise they do
- how many hours they exercise every week
- when they exercise
- where they exercise.

Writing

9 Write a report based on your interviews. Use the extracts in Exercise 3 to help you. Make sure your report has an introduction and conclusion, and includes information about your method, procedure and findings.

> ▶ **Get real**
> Look at some newspapers or business magazines to find an article which gives the findings of a report. Make notes of the subject of the report, its method, procedure and findings. Tell the class about the report.

Before you start

1 What is marketing? Why is it important?

Reading

2 Read this article about marketing. Match the questions (1–6) with the paragraphs (a–f).

1 How do I meet my objectives? ☐
2 What do I want to achieve? ☐
3 What is marketing? ☐
4 How do I communicate my message? ☐
5 How do I find out this information? ☐
6 What do I need to know? ☐

a Marketing is finding out about your customers and competitors so that you can provide the right product at the right price.

b Think about the people you want to sell to: your target market. Different products have different target markets, for example, Swatch and Rolex watches. Questions to ask are:
• Who are my customers – age, sex, income?
• What is the size of the market?
• Is it possible for the market to get bigger?
• What about product awareness – do people know about my company's products?

c You find out this information through market research. Market research uses interviews to find out about people's attitudes and questionnaires to find out about their shopping habits.

d When you know who your customers are and how big your market is, the next step is to set your objectives. Do you want to increase sales? To increase market share? Or to make your product different from the competition?

e Next, think about your strategy for meeting your objectives. If your objective is to increase market share, you could:
• find new customers by making your product more attractive
• take customers from your competitors
• persuade your customers to use more of your product.

f How will you make your strategy work? What message do you want to send? There are many types of promotion and it's important to choose the right one, e.g.
• advertising on TV, in newspapers, etc.
• direct marketing by post (mailshots)
• telesales – selling to customers on the phone
• point-of-sale material in shops – free samples or special offers.
Now you are ready to launch your product in the market. Good luck!

Vocabulary

3 Match the highlighted words and phrases in the text with the definitions (1–8).

1 ways of telling people about your products
_____

2 the part of the total market that buys your products _____

3 knowledge of your company's products
_____

4 other companies that sell similar products
_____

5 finding out about the market _____
6 to introduce a new product to the market
_____

7 the kind of people you are interested in selling to _____

8 a plan you use in order to achieve something
_____

4 Look at the text again. Find and <u>underline</u>:
1 two market research methods
2 three marketing objectives.

Speaking

5 Work in pairs. Take turns to describe the marketing process. Use these phrases:

> First you have to … ■ Then … ■ Next …
> ■ After that … ■ Finally …

6 Work in groups. Think of a product you would like to produce and sell. It could be a new kind of drink or snack or a new range of make-up. You decide. Give your product a name.

Writing

7 You have completed the process in Exercise 5 and are ready to market your product from Exercise 6. Draw up a marketing report with information under these headings. Then present your report.

Product name:
Target market:
Objective:
Strategy:
Promotion:

> ▶ *Get real*
> Do some research. Think of a product you know or buy regularly, and about how the company markets it. Who is their target market? What are their objectives? Find out what you can about the company. What is their market share? Who are their competitors? Tell the class.

21 Advertising and promotion

Before you start

1 Look at these different ways of advertising and answer the questions.

1 Which do you think is best for contacting specific customers?
2 Which do you think is the most expensive?

2 Which way (or ways) of advertising do you think is most suitable for these situations?

1 a travel company selling last-minute trips
2 a car company launching a new model
3 a bank telling customers about a new kind of bank account
4 a local politician who wants people to vote for him/her

Reading

3 Read the business advice information (right). Match the questions (1–4) with the paragraphs (a–d).

1 What does it say? ☐
2 Why are you advertising? ☐
3 Where will you advertise? ☐
4 Who is it for? ☐

Speaking

4 Work in pairs. Read the TALKABOUT advertisement and discuss the questions.

1 What product is the advertisement for?
2 Who are the customers?
3 What is the purpose of the advertisement?
4 What is the message?
5 What is the method?

Writing

5 Look back at the marketing report you did in Unit 20, Exercise 7. Work in groups and design an advertisement for the product. Make sure your advertisement:

• is appropriate for the product and the customer
• has a clear purpose
• has a clear message
• is in the right place.

▶ Get real

Collect some advertisements from newspapers, magazines or direct mail. Choose one you think is good and present it to the class. Say why you think it is good. Make a class display of good advertising material.

Choosing the right advertising for your product or service is really important. Here are some tips.

ⓐ Understand your customers. Find out who they are (their age, interests, lifestyle, income, buying habits). Find out what is the best way to reach them. Which newspapers do they read? Which TV programmes do they watch?

ⓑ What do you want your advertising to achieve? What is its purpose? Do you want to inform people about your product or service? Do you want them to buy it, or see it in a different way? What is its USP (unique selling point)?

ⓒ Keep your message simple and clear. Say just one thing, e.g. 'This is new,' 'This is better,' 'This makes life easier.' Make sure you have a headline that is eye-catching. Make sure the text tells the customer everything you want them to know.

ⓓ Choose a method that will reach your target market. It's no good having a brilliant advertisement if the right people don't see it. It's useless to tell five million people about something that only 100,000 people need to know: banks don't use TV to tell existing customers about a new kind of account.

Go the distance

Stay totally in touch with Motorola's TALKABOUT two-way radio. Wherever your sport takes you – on the ski slopes, in the forest, on the water or in the air – you're in constant contact with your friends or your guide for up to three kilometres. It's simple to use, light and water resistant. And with hands-free and voice activation, it works wherever you choose to take it.

Stay in touch with TALKABOUT. It's made for you.

22 Preparing a presentation

Before you start

1 Have you ever had to speak in front of a large group of people? How did you feel?

2 Work in pairs. What is a presentation? Why do people make presentations? List some reasons.

Reading

3 Here are some 'rules' for preparing a presentation. Match the first sentence of each paragraph (1–6) with the paragraphs (a–f).

1 Decide what you want to say to your audience. ☐

2 Choose the right equipment to help make your talk interesting. ☐

3 Find out who you are talking to. ☐

4 Practise your presentation in advance. ☐

5 Make sure your presentation has a clear structure. ☐

6 Find out about the room you are talking in. ☐

a It's important to know your audience. How many people are there? Where are they from? What do they want to learn? How much do they already know?

b The venue is important too. If possible, visit it before your presentation. Where will the audience sit? Where will you stand? Where will you put your equipment?

c Make sure your objectives are clear. This will help you to prepare material that is interesting and informative. Remember, you want your audience to learn something they don't know. You also want them to enjoy your presentation.

d A well-organized presentation is easier to understand. Give it a beginning, a middle and an end. Make separate points and number them. This structure will help your audience to follow what you are saying.

e There are many different kinds of AV (audio-visual) aids. You can use a simple flip chart or show slides on an overhead projector. There is also computer software, like Microsoft Powerpoint™, which can make your presentation look professional. Choose AV aids that are appropriate for your audience. And make sure you know how they work.

f Make notes of the most important points. Make sure you speak to your audience – don't read to them. Practise giving your talk out loud and check how much time it takes. Ask a friend to listen and give you feedback.

Vocabulary

4 Complete the sentences with the words and phrases from the box.

> appropriate ■ audience ■ AV aids ■ feedback
> ■ informative ■ objectives ■ structure

1 Make sure your presentation is _____ – most people want to learn something new.

2 Your presentation will be easy to understand if it has a clear _____.

3 I'm very nervous; there are over a hundred people in the _____.

4 At the start, explain your _____ so people know why you are talking to them.

5 Knowing your audience will help you choose material that is _____ for their interests.

6 Using _____ is a good way to help communicate your ideas.

7 If you want to know if your presentation was interesting, ask the audience for their _____.

Speaking

5 Work in pairs and do the following:

1 Think of something that you would like to give a presentation about, e.g. a hobby or sport, a place you know well or a subject you are interested in. Decide who you will give it to, and where. (You choose.)

2 Make a list of things to think about when planning a presentation. Discuss each point and make brief notes about it on a piece of paper.

Writing

6 Imagine you have to give your presentation tomorrow. Make more detailed notes about each of the points in Exercise 5. Think about what you will say. Remember, if you read your presentation, it won't sound natural. Make notes to help you speak naturally.

▶ *Get real*

Talk to someone who has given a presentation. What was it about? Did they think it was a good presentation? Why/Why not? What advice would they give someone about preparing a presentation? Report back to the class.

23 Giving a presentation

Before you start

1 You have to give a presentation. Here are some things to do at the beginning of a presentation. Number them in the order you would do them.

a Introduce the main points one by one. ☐

b Welcome the audience. ☐

c Introduce the first point. ☐

d Tell the audience the subject of the presentation. ☐

Reading

2 Read this short introduction to a presentation. Check your answer to Exercise 1.

'Good morning, everyone. It's nice to see so many of you here today. I hope you can all hear me OK.

The subject of my presentation today is our marketing plan for the next three years. Basically, there are three main points I want to talk about. If you look at the first slide, you can see them listed there. First, I'm going to tell you about our new product range aimed at the teenage market. Secondly, I'll talk about each of the products and our plans for marketing them. And finally, I'd like to talk briefly about the competition.

OK, let's start with the first point, our new product range ...'

3 Find and <u>underline</u> the phrases that the speaker uses to do the things in Exercise 1.

Vocabulary

4 The speaker used these phrases in the rest of the presentation. Write the number of each phrase under the correct heading.

1 Thank you for listening.

2 Let's move on to ...

3 Are there any questions?

4 This diagram shows ...

5 So, in conclusion ...

6 As you can see ...

7 My next point is ...

8 If you look at the next slide ...

Connecting the points _____

Referring to AV aids   _____

Finishing   _____

Speaking

5 Work in pairs. Take turns to read the introduction from Exercise 2 aloud.

6 Work in pairs. Look at some ways of ending a presentation. Which ones do you think are good ways of ending? Which are not good? Why?

1 Ask the audience if they have any questions.

2 Stop talking, say goodbye and leave.

3 Write a list of the main points of your talk on the board/flip chart.

4 Thank the audience for coming.

5 Give a very brief summary of what you said and how you feel you achieved your objectives.

6 Give handouts to the audience with the main points of your talk on them.

7 If possible, tell the audience where you will be for the next few minutes so that individuals can come and speak to you.

8 Ask the audience if they have any criticisms of your talk.

Writing

7 Look back at the notes you made in Exercise 6 of Unit 22. Prepare a short introduction for your presentation. Use the introduction in Exercise 2 to help you.

Speaking

8 Work in groups. You are going to give your presentation from Exercise 6 of Unit 22. Use the information on introductions and conclusions in this unit and follow these steps.

• Plan what you are going to say.

• Practise your presentation with a friend.

• Ask your friend to give you feedback.

• Give your presentation to some other students.

▶ **Get real**

Go to a presentation or talk in your school/town. Make notes of the way the speaker introduces and concludes the presentation. Did they help you to follow the points he/she was trying to make? Could you improve on it? How?

Before you start

1 What famous brands (e.g. Nike, Swatch) do you know and what do they sell?

Reading

2 Read Parts A and B of the text quickly. Does the text come from an e-mail, a newspaper article or an advertisement?

Part A

Big companies spend millions of dollars on developing their brand and designing their logo. Market research shows that more and more people are paying attention to the brand of the things they buy. Why? Because global brands like Pepsi have ideas and values connected with them.

Some people are very loyal to one brand because of the ideas and values associated with it. For example, some makes of car are associated with quality or reliability.

Other people are buying an image of themselves – the brand you use says what kind of person you are. Drinking Pepsi Max means you want to get the most from life – you want freedom and adventure, and therefore you are an exciting person. Wearing Nike trainers or sports clothes is all about individual achievement; you can do anything you want – just do it.

Part B

We asked some brand-conscious shoppers what brands they buy, and why.

Kate, 16: I wear these trainers because all my friends wear them. It's important to be cool.

Tom, 27: This car tells people I'm successful. My business clients expect me to drive an expensive car. It gives me the right professional image.

Jane, 20: Yes, it's the latest model. It's got lots of new features and I love the design. I use it to text my friends or call my boyfriend.

3 Read the text again and answer the questions.

Part A

1 Why do big companies spend a lot of money on brands?

2 Why do people buy a particular brand?

Part B

3 Can you guess which brands the three people are talking about?

4 What values or image do they associate with their brand?

Vocabulary

4 Match the words and phrases from the article (1–6) with the definitions (a–f). Then write the words and phrases in your language.

1 logo   ☐ _____
2 values   ☐ _____
3 loyal   ☐ _____
4 image   ☐ _____
5 individual achievement   ☐ _____
6 brand-conscious   ☐ _____

a the general impression you give to other people
b something you do successfully, on your own
c aware of different brands and what they represent
d not changing, always buying the same brand
e things that are important or that you believe in
f symbol that appears on a company's products

Speaking

5 Work in pairs. Are you brand-conscious? Discuss these questions.

- Are brands important to you?
- What brands do you buy?
- What values do you associate with them?
- What image do you want other people to have of you?
- Are there any brands you would not buy?

Writing

6 Design your own brand. Think of a product – anything you like. What ideas and values do you want to be associated with it? Give it a name and design a logo.

 Get real

Research a brand that you are familiar with and that you think has good values associated with it. Find more information about it using magazines or the Internet. Explain your brand to the class and say why you think it's successful.

25 Profit at any price?

Before you start

1 Read these two quotes about a company's responsibilities. Which one is closer to your opinion?

1 In business, profits are more important than people.
2 A company must look after its customers first, its workers second, and its shareholders last.

Reading

2 Work in pairs. Read about the activities of two companies. One student reads Part A. The other student reads Part B. Answer the questions for your text. Then tell your partner about the company.

1 Why is the activity good for business?
2 What is the problem with each activity?
3 What *pressure group* is mentioned? What does it do?

Part A

For many years, sales of cigarettes in western countries have been falling, because people know more about the dangers of smoking. Because of this, one large tobacco company has increased its marketing activities in Asia and Latin America. In these parts of the world, people know less about the danger to their health from smoking. At the moment, about 150,000 people a year in Latin America die from smoking-related illness. This number is going up every year. The tobacco company knows this, but it continues to sell more and more cigarettes in these countries. The pressure group ASH (Action on Smoking and Health) says tobacco companies use the fact that people don't understand the dangers. They believe this is unethical as it puts profits before people.

Part B

Each year, farmers in Africa and Asia sell most of their crops (e.g. rice, corn), but save a small amount to grow the next year. Now, a US company has developed a new plant gene called the Terminator. If a plant has this gene, it produces seeds which won't grow again after the first year. This means the farmers must buy new seeds every year. This is good for the company's profits. But pressure groups like Greenpeace say this is irresponsible. They say that it kills the natural plants and means farmers have to get their seeds from the company. If farmers can't afford to buy the company's seeds, they will have no crops to grow. The result could be that people die from hunger.

Vocabulary

3 Underline words in the article that mean:

1 not ethical   2 not responsible.

4 Choose a prefix (*in-*, *im-*, *il-*, *ir-*, *un-*) to make the opposite of these adjectives.

1 acceptable _____   4 polite _____
2 correct _____   5 regular _____
3 legal _____

Speaking

5 Work in pairs. Look at the information below and discuss the questions.

1 Which option is better for:
  a the customers?
  b workers in the United States?
  c workers in Indonesia?
  d the shareholders?

2 Is it ethical to exploit the low cost of labour in Indonesia? Why/Why not?
3 What do you think Company X should do?

Company X produces sports shoes. It has factories in the US, but labour costs in the US are high. This means its shoes are very expensive. The company is thinking about moving its manufacturing operation to Indonesia, where labour costs are very low.

	Option 1: manufacturing in the US	Option 2: manufacturing in Indonesia
for the customers	more expensive shoes	cheaper shoes
for workers in the US	jobs with good pay/conditions	lose their jobs
for workers in Indonesia	no new jobs	jobs with low pay, long hours, bad conditions
for the shareholders	lower profits, company is not competitive	higher profits, company is very competitive

▶ ## Get real

Work as a class. Use the Internet, magazines, newspapers or TV programmes to find stories about 'unethical' companies and their activities. Report back to the class. Make a list of the most unacceptable things the companies do and discuss what you might do about them.

Before you start

1 When you apply for a job, you write a letter of application. What information should you put into your letter? Make a list.

Reading

2 Look at this advert. Would you like this 'job'?

> ### Crew members wanted
>
> We are planning an expedition to sail the Atlantic Ocean in a replica of the ship used by Christopher Columbus in 1492. We are looking for two young, fit and enthusiastic people to join our crew. You need to be hard-working, flexible and good at working in a team. Travel experience is essential. Experience of sailing would be an advantage. We offer a unique opportunity for the right people. Apply in writing, with your CV, to: jim.smith@realitytv.co.uk.

3 Read this advice for writing a letter of application and the letter from Helen King. Is Helen right for the 'job'? Does she follow the advice?

> 1 Read the advertisement. Think about exactly what kind of person the organization wants.
>
> 2 Look at the personal qualities (e.g. hard-working, enthusiastic) and the experience they ask for. Talk about them in your letter.
>
> 3 Your letter should be polite and formal:
> • say where you saw the advertisement
> • say why you are applying
> • give a short summary of your experience
> • talk about personal qualities
> • include a closing statement.

Dear Mr Smith

¹ ___ your advertisement for crew members in The Times. I would like to apply for the post, and enclose a copy of my CV for your attention.
² ___ my personal qualities and experience make me an excellent candidate for this post. ³ ___, I have three years' experience of working on charity projects in developing countries. On these projects, I worked with people from different backgrounds, both independently and as part of a team. I learned to carry out my responsibilities but also to look after the needs of others in the team.
⁴ ___ very much sailing experience, but ⁵ ___ learn. I am highly motivated, hard-working and very well organized. These are all qualities which enabled me to succeed in my charity work. I am sure they will make me a key member of your crew.
I hope you will consider my application. ⁶ ___ contact me if you need more information.
⁷ ___ hearing from you.

Yours sincerely

Helen King

4 Match the gaps (1–7) in the letter with the phrases (a–g).

a As you can see from my CV
b I am willing to
c I believe that
d I look forward to
e I do not have
f I am writing in response to
g Please do not hesitate to

Vocabulary

5 Complete the definitions with the highlighted words from the advert and the advice.

1 _____ means very unusual.
2 An _____ helps you do better than other people.
3 _____ means very important or necessary.
4 A _____ is a short description of something, with no detail.
5 _____ means serious and businesslike.

6 *Hard-working* and *enthusiastic* are two personal qualities. Find and underline some others in the advert and letter. Use the Glossary or a dictionary to find the words in your language.

Writing

7 You want to apply for the job in the advert below. Make a list of your personal qualities. Invent experience that would be useful for the job, then write a letter applying for the job.

> ### Holiday helpers for disabled children
>
> We are looking for enthusiastic people aged 16–18 to work as helpers on activity holidays for disabled children. The children we work with are aged between 8 and 11, and these holidays give them the chance for new experiences, such as horse-riding, sailing and swimming. You need to have lots of energy and enjoy working in a team. Experience of working with children would be an advantage, but is not essential.
>
> We offer a weekly allowance, free accommodation and the chance to do something really important.
>
> Apply in writing, with your CV, to: alison@summerkids.com.

▶ ### Get real
Find a job advertisement in your own language or invent one. Translate it into English. Give it to a friend and ask them to write a letter applying for it. Write an application letter for the job advertisement they give you.

27 Team working

Before you start

1 Take the quiz. Be honest! Then look at the answers on page 40 to find out if you are a team player.

> ### Are you a team player?
>
> **1 Do you prefer:**
> A team sports like soccer and basketball?
> B individual sports like swimming and cycling?
>
> **2 When you have a free evening, do you prefer to:**
> A go out with friends?
> B stay at home watching TV?
>
> **3 If your school put on a play, would you be:**
> A in the cast? B in the audience?
>
> **4 If your teacher gives you a group project, do you:**
> A suggest your group meets after school to share ideas?
> B go home and work on your own ideas?
>
> **5 Is your ideal activity on a sunny weekend:**
> A a picnic with friends at the beach?
> B a long walk in the country?

Reading

2 Read the information about *Eco-challenge*. Would you like to be part of an Eco-challenge team? Why/Why not?

> ### Eco-challenge
>
> *Eco-challenge* is one of the toughest races in the world. Teams of four people complete a number of activities over a 200-km route. These include kayaking, mountain-biking, climbing, and jungle trekking. The race takes six days. The teams carry all their own food, water, and equipment. The winning team is the one that completes all the stages in the fastest time.

3 Read the quotes from two members of an Eco-challenge team and complete the lists with words or phrases from the quotes.

> ### Andy (team leader)
>
> *Eco-challenge* is very tiring. You need to be fit and to have a lot of stamina. As leader, you have to be able to work with other people and you must want to succeed. I need to be positive all the time. I'm responsible for making sure the team works together. I need to make decisions, to give encouragement and to help bring out the best in the team members.

> ### Jenna (team member)
>
> You're part of a team. It's sometimes difficult to be unselfish when you're tired and stressed, but the only way to succeed is to work together. You must have total commitment to the team's success, so cooperation is really important. You have to be supportive, especially if one person is having problems. Sometimes things go wrong and you have to solve the problem; it's important to be resourceful.

You need to be	You need to be able to	You need to have
fit	work with other people	stamina
_____	_____	_____
_____	_____	_____

Vocabulary

4 Complete the lists with nouns and adjectives from the quotes in Exercise 3.

noun	adjective
_____	committed
_____	cooperative
_____	encouraging
resourcefulness	
responsibility	_____
_____	successful
support	_____

Speaking

5 You are putting together a team to enter a 'school challenge', competing against other schools. Read the information and discuss the questions.

1 What qualities will they need?
2 Who should represent your school?

> ### School Challenge Saturday 14th July
>
> **A fun day of races and competitions**
> **All events are for teams of four people.**
> **Events include:**
> - mini-triathlon (running 1km, swimming 100m, cycling 5km)
> - skateboarding
> - problem-solving
> - quizzes, games and lots more.
>
> **First prize (winning team):** €2,000
> **Second prize:** €1,000
> **Ten further prizes of** €500

> ### ▶ Get real
>
> Interview someone who has experience of being in a team, e.g. at work, in sport, for a charity event. Find out what they think makes a good team player. Report back to the class.

Before you start

1 Look at the dictionary definitions. What kind of things do you have to negotiate, e.g. with your parents (the amount of pocket money you get or when you have to be home in the evening) or with your teacher (homework schedules)?

> **negotiate** /nɪˈgəʊʃieɪt/ **verb** 1 [I] **negotiate (with sb) (for/about sth)** to talk to sb in order to decide or agree about sth

> **negotiation** /nɪˌgəʊʃiˈeɪʃn/ **noun** [C, often pl, U] a formal discussion at which people try to decide or agree sth

(Entries taken from the Oxford Wordpower Dictionary)

Reading

2 Read this introduction to negotiating and answer the questions.

  1 What makes a good negotiation?
  2 What makes a good negotiator?

A successful negotiation is when two people (or teams) reach agreement on something which they are both happy with. There should not be a winner and a loser. The negotiation should end with both people getting what they want (win-win). For example, if workers negotiate with the company's management, the workers may get more pay and the management may get better productivity.

To be a good negotiator takes a lot of skill and preparation. You need to:

- understand what is a good result for the other team as well as yourself
- have a clear idea of your objectives
- be willing to compromise on your objectives
- be sure what your priorities are – what is most important to you
- have a strategy – a plan of what you are going to do and say
- listen carefully to the other people – what they say, and how they say it
- be well-prepared.

Vocabulary

3 <u>Underline</u> the words in the text that mean:

  1 accept less than you want in order to reach agreement
  2 the final situation at the end of the discussion
  3 a plan that you use to achieve something
  4 the most important things you want to do

4 Look at these stages in a negotiation. Number them in the order that seems most logical to you.

Bargaining – discussing the terms – a process of 'give and take' ☐

Preparation – thinking about what both sides want ☐

Concluding – agreeing, making sure everyone is happy ☐

Proposals – each side makes and responds to suggestions ☐

Stating positions – both sides explain what they want from the negotiation ☐

Reading

5 Some students are organizing a charity concert. Read the three extracts on page 33 from a negotiation between the students and the manager of the local community centre. Match the extracts with *three* of the stages in Exercise 4. (S = student representative, M = community centre manager)

Vocabulary

6 Put the phrases in italics from the dialogue under the correct headings.

Stating your position

_____
_____
_____
_____

Showing you understand the other person's position

_____
_____

Making proposals

_____
_____
_____

Responding to proposals

_____
_____
_____

Bargaining

_____
_____
_____
_____

The situation

The students are organizing the concert to support Greenpeace, a charity for the environment. They want to use the hall at the centre for free. The community centre has financial problems and the manager needs to make money out of every event.

Extract 1 _____

S *... OK, our position is this. We want to* make as much money as possible for Greenpeace. We're charging six euros a ticket. All the people taking part in the concert are performing for free. *The problem is,* if we have to pay you to use the hall, we'll have less money for Greenpeace.

M *Yes, I see your point.* But *my situation is this.* A concert in the hall will use electricity, and one of my staff will need to be there. *I have to* pay for these. *I need to* make sure that I cover my costs. Also, the community centre needs to make money too.

S *OK, I understand that,* but ...

Extract 2 _____

M ... *What I'd like to suggest* is that we discuss the possibility of you paying us something towards the cost of using the hall, but not the entire cost.

S *OK, that seems reasonable. Why don't you* work out exactly how much you think it will cost? Then we can discuss it.

M *Yes, that's a good idea.* And *maybe we could discuss* a donation to the community centre as well?

S Hmm ... *I'm not sure about that ...*

Extract 3 _____

M ... *If you pay us* 20 per cent of the money you take, *we'll let you* use the hall.

S That seems rather high. I'm not sure I can agree to that.

M *If you agree, we'll let you* use the café to sell coffee and soft drinks.

S That sounds possible. *How about if we pay you* 15 per cent of the money for the tickets? And *we'll also pay you* 25 per cent of the profits from the coffee and soft drinks ...

Speaking

7 Work in groups of four. Divide into pairs, Team A and Team B. Negotiate to find a solution to the problem below. Remember, you want a win-win result.

Team A: It is the basketball season. You belong to the school basketball club. You practise three afternoons a week in the school gym between 4.00 and 5.30 p.m. The gym is locked at 5.30 and closed on Fridays. But the head teacher has told the school drama society that it can use the gym after school as well. Your training sessions are very important. You have a big competition coming up in two weeks' time and the gym is the only place you can train.

Team B: You belong to the school drama society. You are putting on a musical in three weeks' time. You need somewhere to rehearse after school for the next three weeks and the head teacher has told you can use the school gym. Unfortunately, the basketball club uses the gym three afternoons a week between the end of school and 5.30. You don't have anywhere else to rehearse and you need to rehearse every day from now until you put the musical on.

> ### Get real
>
> **Work as a class.** Use business books or magazines to find out about negotiating styles in your country. Do people look for a win-win result or do they prefer win-lose? Can you think of a recent situation where there have been negotiations in your country, e.g. public service salary reviews? What was the result? Report back to the class.

Glossary

Short forms

[C]	countable	*adv*	adverb
[U]	uncountable	*prep*	preposition
[pl]	plural	*sb*	somebody
adj	adjective	*sth*	something

A

acceptable /ək'septəbl/ *adj* agreed or approved of by most people in society (opposite: **unacceptable**)

account /ə'kaʊnt/ *noun* [C] a record of all the money that a person or business has received or paid out

achieve /ə'tʃiːv/ *verb* to gain sth, usually by hard work or skill

achievement /ə'tʃiːvmənt/ *noun* [C, U] something that you have done successfully, especially through hard work or skill

acronym /'ækrənɪm/ *noun* [C] a short word that is made from the first letters of a group of words

action point /'ækʃn pɔɪnt/ *noun* [C] something which is mentioned at a meeting and noted down to be dealt with or done later

adapt /ə'dæpt/ *verb* to change sth so that you can use it in a different situation

advantage /əd'vɑːntɪdʒ/ *noun* [C] something that may help you to do better than other people

advertise /'ædvətaɪz/ *verb* to put information on television, on a picture on the wall, etc. in order to persuade people to buy sth
➤ **advertising** /'ædvətaɪzɪŋ/ *noun* [U] **advertisement** /əd'vɜːtɪsmənt/ (also informal **advert** /'ædvɜːt/ **ad** /æd/) *noun* [C] a piece of information in a newspaper, on television, etc. that tries to persuade people to buy sth, to interest them in a new job, etc.

afford /ə'fɔːd/ *verb* to have enough money or time to be able to do sth

agenda /ə'dʒendə/ *noun* [C] a list of things that will happen or be discussed and dealt with at a meeting

aid /eɪd/ *noun* [C] an object, a machine, a tool, etc. that you use to help you do sth

aim /eɪm/ *verb* 1 (**aim sth at sb/sth**) to direct sth at a particular person or group 2 (**aim to do sth**) to intend to do or achieve sth

allow /ə'laʊ/ *verb* to make it possible for sb/sth to do sth

applicant /'æplɪkənt/ *noun* [C] a person who makes a formal request for sth (**applies for sth**), especially for a job, a place at a university, etc.

application /ˌæplɪ'keɪʃn/ *noun* [C,U] a formal written request, especially for a job or a place in a school, club, etc.

apply /ə'plaɪ/ *verb* (**apply (to sb) (for sth)**) to ask for sth in writing

appointment /ə'pɔɪntmənt/ *noun* [C,U] an arrangement to see sb at a particular time

appropriate /ə'prəʊpriət/ *adj* (**appropriate for/to sb/sth**) suitable or right for a particular situation, person, etc.

arrangement /ə'reɪndʒmənt/ *noun* [C, usually pl] plans or preparations for sth that will happen in the future

associate /ə'səʊʃieɪt/ *verb* (**associate sb/sth (with sb/sth)**) to make a connection between people or things in your mind

attach /ə'tætʃ/ *verb* to fasten or join a document, etc. to an e-mail
➤ **attached** /ə'tætʃt/ *adj*

attend /ə'tend/ *verb* to go to or be present at a place

audience /'ɔːdiəns/ *noun* [C] all the people who are watching or listening to a play, concert, speech, the television, etc.

audio-visual /ˌɔːdiəʊ 'vɪʒuəl/ *adj* using both sound and pictures

B

bar chart /'bɑː tʃɑːt/ *noun* [C] a diagram which uses narrow bands of different heights to show different amounts, so that they can be compared

bargain /'bɑːgən/ *verb* (**bargain (with sb) (about/over/for sth)**) to discuss prices, conditions, etc. with sb in order to reach an agreement that suits each person

battery /'bætri; -təri/ *noun* [C] a device which provides electricity for a toy, radio, car, etc.

benefit /'benɪfɪt/ *noun* [C, usually pl] advantages that you get from your company in addition to the money you earn

billboard /'bɪlbɔːd/ *noun* [C] a large board on the outside of a building or at the side of the road, used for putting advertisements on

bonus /'bəʊnəs/ *noun* [C] an extra amount of money that is added to sb's wages as a reward

boring /'bɔːrɪŋ/ *adj* not at all interesting; dull

bow /baʊ/ *verb* to bend your head or the top part of your body forward and down, as a sign of respect

brainstorm /'breɪnstɔːm/ *verb* to solve a problem or make a decision by thinking of as many ideas as possible in a short time

brand /brænd/ *noun* [C] the name of a product that is made by a particular company

brand-conscious /'brænd kɒnʃəs/ *adj* aware of the different types of product made by different companies and what each one represents

btw (*abbr*) used in writing to mean 'by the way'

budget /'bʌdʒɪt/ *noun* [C] the amount of money that is available to be spent on a particular task or activity

build /bɪld/ *verb* to make sth by putting pieces, materials, etc. together

business /'bɪznəs/ *noun* [C] a firm, a shop, a factory, etc. which produces or sells goods or provides a service

business card (also **card**) /'bɪznəs kɑːd/ *noun* [C] a small card printed with sb's name and details of his/her job and company

business class /'bɪznəs klɑːs/ *noun* [U] the more expensive and comfortable seats on a plane, train, etc., which are designed for people travelling on business

businesslike /'bɪznəslaɪk/ *adj* (used about a person) working in an efficient and organized way and not wasting time

businessman, businesswoman /'bɪznəsmæn/; /'bɪznəswʊmən/ *noun* [C] a person who works in business, especially at a high level

busy /'bɪzi/ *adj* 1 having a lot of work or tasks to do; not free; working on sth 2 (especially US) (used about a telephone) being used

C

calculate /'kælkjuleɪt/ *verb* to find sth out by using mathematics; to work sth out

call (sb) back *phrasal verb* to telephone sb again or to telephone sb who has phoned you earlier

caller /'kɔːlə/ *noun* [C] a person who is making a telephone call

camera operator /'kæmərər ɒpəreɪtə/ *noun* [C] a person whose job is to work the camera and to record everything for a film or a television company

candidate /'kændɪdət; -deɪt/ *noun* [C] a person who makes a formal request to be considered for a job or wants to be elected to a particular position

capital /'kæpɪtl/ *noun* [singular] a large amount of money that is invested or is used to start a business

cater /'keɪtə/ *verb* (**cater for sb/sth**) to provide what sb/sth needs or wants

celebration /ˌselɪ'breɪʃn/ *noun* [C] the act or occasion of doing sth enjoyable because sth good has happened or because it is a special day

CEO /ˌsiː iː ˈəʊ/ = chief executive officer

chairperson /ˈtʃeəpɜːsn/ *noun* [C] **1** the person in charge of a company, an organization, etc. **2** a person who controls or is in charge of a meeting

challenge /ˈtʃælɪndʒ/ *noun* [C] something new and difficult that forces you to make a lot of effort

challenging /ˈtʃælɪndʒɪŋ/ *adj* difficult in an interesting way that tests your ability

charge[1] /tʃɑːdʒ/ *verb* to ask sb to pay a particular amount of money

charge[2] /tʃɑːdʒ/ *noun* [U] (**in charge of sb/sth**) a position of control over sb/sth; responsibility for sb/sth

charity /ˈtʃærəti/ *noun* [C, U] an organization that collects money to help people who are poor, sick, etc. or to do work that is useful to society

chief executive officer /ˌtʃiːf ɪgˈzekjətɪv ɒfɪsə/ *noun* [C] (*abbr* **CEO**) the person with the highest position in a company or an organization

childcare /ˈtʃaɪldkeə/ *noun* [U] the care of children, especially while their parents are at work

client /ˈklaɪənt/ *noun* [C] a person who uses the services or advice of a professional person or an organization

colleague /ˈkɒliːg/ *noun* [C] a person who works at the same place as you

commitment /kəˈmɪtmənt/ *noun* [U] (**to sth**) the willingness to work hard and give a lot of your time and attention to sth because you believe it is right or important ➤ **committed** /kəˈmɪtɪd/ *adj*

communicate /kəˈmjuːnɪkaɪt/ *verb* to share and exchange information, ideas or feelings with sb

company /ˈkʌmpəni/ *noun* [C] a business organization that sells goods or services

company car /ˌkʌmpəni ˈkɑː/ *noun* [C] a car that is provided by the company for your own use while you are working for that company

compare /kəmˈpeə/ *verb* (**compare A with/to B**) to consider people or things in order to see how similar or different they are ➤ **comparison** /kəmˈpærɪsn/ *noun* [C]

compete /kəmˈpiːt/ *verb* to try to win or achieve sth, or to try to be better than sb else ➤ **competitor** /kəmˈpetɪtə/ *noun* [C] a person or an organization that is competing against others

the competition /ˌkɒmpəˈtɪʃn/ *noun* [singular] the other people, companies, etc. who are trying to achieve the same thing as you

competitive /kəmˈpetətɪv/ *adj* able to be as successful as or more successful than others
➤ **competitiveness** *noun* [U]

complaint /kəmˈpleɪnt/ *noun* [C] a statement that you are not satisfied with or happy about sth

compromise /ˈkɒmprəmaɪz/ *verb* (**compromise (with sb) (on sth)**) to accept less than you want or are aiming for, especially in order to reach an agreement

conclude /kənˈkluːd/ *verb* to end or to bring sth to an end

conclusion /kənˈkluːʒn/ *noun* [C] something that you decide when you have thought about all the information connected with the situation

confident /ˈkɒnfɪdənt/ *adj* feeling or showing that you are sure about your own abilities, opinions, etc.

conditions /kənˈdɪʃnz/ *noun* [pl] the circumstances and situation in which people live, work or do things

confirm /kənˈfɜːm/ *verb* to say or show that sth is true; to make sth definite

consist of sth *phrasal verb* to be formed or made up of sb/sth

control panel /kənˈtrəʊl pænl/ *noun* [C] a flat board in a vehicle or on a piece of machinery where the controls and instruments are fixed

co-operation /kəʊˌɒpəˈreɪʃn/ *noun* [U] the fact of doing sth or working together with sb else to achieve sth
➤ **co-operative** /kəʊˈɒpərətɪv/ *adj*

correct /kəˈrekt/ *adj* suitable, proper or right (opposite: **incorrect**)

costs /kɒsts/ *noun* [pl] the total amount of money that needs to be spent by a business

covering letter /ˌkʌvərɪŋ ˈletə/ *noun* [C] a letter containing extra information about yourself that you send with sth, especially a job application

create /kriˈeɪt/ *verb* to make sth new happen or exist

creative /kriˈeɪtɪv/ *adj* using skill or imagination to make or do new things

crew /kruː/ *noun* [C] **1** all the people who work on a ship, aircraft, etc. **2** a group of people with special technical skills who work together, especially in film making

criticism /ˈkrɪtɪsɪzəm/ *noun* [C, U] (an expression of) what you think is bad about sb/sth

currency /ˈkʌrənsi/ *noun* [C, U] the system or type of money that a particular country uses

curriculum vitae /kəˌrɪkjələm ˈviːtaɪ/ = CV

customer /ˈkʌstəmə/ *noun* [C] a person who buys goods or services in a shop, restaurant, etc.

customer services /ˌkʌstəmə ˈsɜːvɪsɪz/ *noun* [U] the department in a company that deals with customers and takes their orders

CV /ˌsiː ˈviː/ *noun* [singular] curriculum vitae; a formal list of your education and work experience, often used when you are trying to get a new job

D

data /ˈdeɪtə/ *noun* [U, pl] facts or information

deal with sth *phrasal verb* to take suitable action in a particular situation in order to solve a problem, complete a task, etc.

demand /dɪˈmɑːnd/ *noun* [U,C] the desire or need of customers for goods or services which they want to buy or use

design[1] /dɪˈzaɪn/ *verb* to invent, plan and develop sth for a particular purpose

design[2] /dɪˈzaɪn/ *noun* **1** [C] a drawing or plan that shows how sth should be made, built, etc. **2** [U] the way in which sth is planned and made or arranged

develop /dɪˈveləp/ *verb* **1** to gradually grow or become bigger, stronger, etc. **2** to make sth bigger, better, more advanced, etc.

device /dɪˈvaɪs/ *noun* [C] a tool or piece of equipment made for a particular purpose

difficult /ˈdɪfɪkəlt/ *adj* not easy to do or understand

direct marketing /dəˌrekt ˈmɑːkɪtɪŋ/ *noun* [U] the business of selling products or services directly to customers who order by mail or by telephone instead of going to a shop

director /dəˈrektə, daɪ-, dɪ-/ *noun* [C] **1** one of a group of senior managers who control or run a company **2** a person in charge of a film or play who tells the actors and staff what to do

display[1] /dɪˈspleɪ/ *noun* [C] an arrangement of things in a public place for people to see

display[2] /dɪˈspleɪ/ *verb* (used about a computer, etc.) to show information

distribute /dɪˈstrɪbjuːt/ *verb* to transport and supply goods to shops, companies, etc.

distribution /ˌdɪstrɪˈbjuːʃn/ *noun* **1** [singular, U] the act of transporting and delivering goods to clients **2** [U] the department in a company that is responsible for transporting and delivering goods to clients

DJ /ˈdiː dʒeɪ/ (also **disc jockey** /ˈdɪsk dʒɒki/) *noun* [C] a person who plays records, CDs, etc. and talks about music on the radio or in a club

dos and don'ts /ˌduːz ən ˈdəʊnts/ *idiom* rules that you should follow

document /ˈdɒkjument/ *noun* [C] an official piece of writing which gives information, proof or evidence

donation /dəʊˈneɪʃn/ *noun* [C] money, etc. that is given to a person or an organization such as a charity, in order to help people or animals in need

double /ˈdʌbl/ *adj, determiner* twice as much or as many as usual

E

earn /ɜːn/ *verb* to get money by working

education /ˌedʒuˈkeɪʃn/ *noun* [C, U] the teaching or training of people, especially in schools

electrician /ɪˌlekˈtrɪʃn/ *noun* [C] a person whose job is to connect, repair, etc. electrical equipment

e-mail /ˈiːmeɪl/ *noun* [C, U] a way of sending messages to other people by means of computers connected together in a network; a message sent in this way

emoticon /ɪˈməʊtɪkɒn/ *noun* [C] a group of keyboard symbols that are used to show how you feel at the time of writing an e-mail or text message, e.g. :-) represents a smiling face

employ /ɪmˈplɔɪ/ *verb* to pay sb to work for you

employee /ɪmˈplɔɪiː/ *noun* [C] a person who is paid to work for sb else

employment /ɪmˈplɔɪmənt/ *noun* [U] the state of having a paid job

enable /ɪˈneɪbl/ *verb* (**enable sb/sth to do sth**) to make it possible for sb/sth to do sth

enclose /ɪnˈkləʊz/ *verb* to put sth in an envelope, package, etc. with sth else

encouragement /ɪnˈkʌrɪdʒmənt/ *noun* [U, C] the act of giving sb hope, support or the confidence to do sth ➤ **encouraging** /ɪnˈkʌrɪdʒɪŋ/ *adj*

enthusiastic /ɪnˌθjuːziˈæstɪk/ *adj* full of excitement and interest in sth

entrepreneur /ˌɒntrəprəˈnɜː/ *noun* [C] a person who makes money by starting or running businesses, especially when he/she has to take financial risks

the environment *noun* [singular] the natural world in which people, animals and plants live

equipment /ɪˈkwɪpmənt/ *noun* [U] the things that are needed for a particular purpose or to do an activity

essential /ɪˈsenʃl/ *adj* completely necessary; that you must have or do

ethical /ˈeθɪkl/ *adj* morally correct (opposite: **unethical**)

exchange rate /ɪksˈtʃeɪndʒ reɪt/ *noun* [U, C] the relation in value between kinds of money used in different countries

expedition /ˌekspəˈdɪʃn/ *noun* [C] a long journey that is made for a special purpose

expenses /ɪkˈspensɪz/ *noun* [pl] money that you spend while you are working that your employer will pay back to you later

experience /ɪkˈspɪəriəns/ *noun* [U] the things that you have done in your life; the knowledge or skill that you get from seeing or doing sth

expert /ˈekspɜːt/ *noun* [C] a person who has a lot of special knowledge or skill

export¹ /ˈekspɔːt/ *noun* [C, usually pl] something that is sent to another country for sale

export² /ɪkˈspɔːt/ *verb* to send goods, etc. to another country, usually for sale ➤ **exporter** /ɪkˈspɔːtə/ *noun* [C]

F

fall /fɔːl/ *verb* **1** to drop down towards the ground **2** to become lower or less

familiar /fəˈmɪliə/ *adj* (used about a person's behaviour) too friendly and informal

feedback /ˈfiːdbæk/ *noun* [U] information or comments about sth that you have done which tells you how good or bad it is

finance /ˈfaɪnæns/ *noun* [U] (**finance department**) the department in a company that manages the money that a company has and pays the employees their salaries

finding /ˈfaɪndɪŋ/ *noun* [C, usually pl] information that is discovered as a result of research into sth

fit¹ /fɪt/ *adj* strong and in good physical health (especially because of exercise)

fit² /fɪt/ *verb* to make sth right or suitable for sb/sth

fix /fɪks/ *verb* (esp US) to repair sth

fixed /fɪkst/ *adj* staying the same; not changing or able to be changed

fixed costs /fɪkst ˈkɒsts/ *noun* [pl] the costs that a business must pay that do not change, even if the amount of work produced changes

flexible /ˈfleksəbl/ *adj* **1** (used about a person) able to change to adapt to new conditions or situations **2** able to bend or move easily without breaking

flexible hours /ˌfleksəbl ˈaʊəz/ *noun* [pl] a system in which a worker can choose what time he/she starts or finishes work each day

flip chart /ˈflɪp tʃɑːt/ *noun* [C] large sheets of paper fixed at the top to a stand so that they can be turned over, used for presenting information at a talk or meeting

formal /ˈfɔːml/ *adj* very correct and suitable for official or important occasions (opposite: **informal**)

G

global /ˈgləʊbl/ *adj* covering or affecting the whole world

glove /glʌv/ *noun* [C] a piece of clothing that covers your hand and has five separate parts for the fingers

go down *phrasal verb* to drop or become lower; to decrease

go up *phrasal verb* to rise or become higher; to increase

goods /gʊdz/ *noun* [pl] things that are for sale

graduate /ˈgrædʒuət/ *noun* [C] a person who has a first degree from a university, etc.

graph /græf/ *noun* [C] a diagram in which a line or a curve shows the relationship between two quantities, measurements, etc.

greet /griːt/ *verb* to welcome sb when you meet him/her; to say hello to sb ➤ **greeting** /ˈgriːtɪŋ/ *noun* [C]

grip /grɪp/ *noun* [C] the person whose job is to prepare and move the cameras while a film is being made

H

handout /ˈhændaʊt/ *noun* [C] a free document that is given to a lot of people to advertise sth or explain sth, for example in a class or talk

hard-working /ˌhɑːd ˈwɜːkɪŋ/ *adj* putting a lot of effort into a job and doing it well

headline /ˈhedlaɪn/ *noun* [C] the title of a news article, an advertisement, etc. printed in large letters, especially at the top of the page

the health service /ˈhelθ sɜːvɪs/ *noun* [C] the organization of the medical services of a country

helpful /ˈhelpfl/ *adj* giving, or wanting to give, help

hesitate /ˈhezɪteɪt/ *verb* (**hesitate (to do sth)**) to be worried about doing sth because you are not sure that it is right or appropriate

hold on *phrasal verb* used on the telephone to ask sb to wait until he/she can talk to the person he/she wants to talk to

hug /hʌg/ *verb* to put your arms around sb, especially to show that you love him/her

human resources /ˌhjuːmən rɪˈsɔːsɪz/ *noun* [U] (*abbr* **HR**) the department in a company that deals with employing and training people

I

image /ˈɪmɪdʒ/ *noun* [C] the general impression that a person, an organization or a product, etc. gives to the public

impolite /ˌɪmpəˈlaɪt/ *adj* rude

import /ˈɪmpɔːt/ *noun* [C, usually pl] a product or service that is brought into one country from another

in conclusion /kənˈkluːʒn/ *idiom* finally; lastly

Inc. /ɪŋk/ (*abbr*) Incorporated; used after the name of a company in the US

income /ˈɪŋkʌm/ *noun* [C,U] the amount of money that you receive regularly as payment for your work or as interest on money you have saved, etc.

increase /ɪnˈkriːs/ *verb* to become or make sth larger in number or amount

independent /ˌɪndɪˈpendənt/ *adj* not needing or wanting help
➤ **independently** /-li/ *adv*

individual¹ /ˌɪndɪˈvɪdʒuəl/ *adj* considered separately rather than as part of a group

individual² /ˌɪndɪˈvɪdʒuəl/ *noun* [C] one person, considered separately rather than as part of a group

individuality /ˌɪndɪˌvɪdʒuˈæləti/ *noun* [U] the qualities that make sb/sth different from other people or things

information technology /ˌɪnfəˌmeɪʃn tekˈnɒlədʒi/ *noun* [U] (*abbr* **IT**) the department that looks after the electronic equipment that a company uses, especially its computers

informative /ɪnˈfɔːmətɪv/ *adj* giving useful information

interest /ˈɪntrəst/ *noun* [U] the money that you pay for borrowing money from a bank, etc. or the money that you earn when you keep money in a bank, etc.

interesting /ˈɪntrəstɪŋ/ *adj* enjoyable and not boring; holding your attention

Internet /ˈɪntənet/ (**the Internet/the Net**) *noun* [singular] the international system of computers that makes it possible for you to see information from all around the world on your computer and to send information to other computers

interpreter /ɪnˈtɜːprɪtə/ *noun* [C] a person whose job is to translate what sb is saying into another language as he/she hears it

interrupt /ˌɪntəˈrʌpt/ *verb* to say or do sth that makes sb stop what he/she is saying or doing

interview /ˈɪntəvjuː/ *verb* **1** to ask sb questions to find out if he/she is suitable for a job, course of study, etc. **2** to ask sb questions about his/her opinions, private life, etc., especially on the radio or television or for a newspaper, magazine, etc.

interviewee /ˌɪntəvjuːˈiː/ *noun* [C] a person who is questioned in an interview

introduction /ˌɪntrəˈdʌkʃn/ *noun* **1** [C, usually pl] the act of telling two or more people each others' names for the first time **2** [C] the first part of a book, report, a piece of written work or a talk, which gives a general idea of what is to follow

invent /ɪnˈvent/ *verb* to think of or make sth for the first time

invention /ɪnˈvenʃn/ *noun* [C] a thing that has been made or designed by sb for the first time

invest /ɪnˈvest/ *verb* (**invest (sth) in sth**) to put money into a bank, business, property, etc. in the hope that you will make a profit
➤ **investment** /ɪnˈvestmənt/ *noun* [U, C]

irresponsible /ˌɪrɪˈspɒnsəbl/ *adj* not thinking about the effect your actions will have; not showing a feeling of responsibility

J

job satisfaction /ˈdʒɒb sætɪsfækʃn/ *noun* [U] the good feeling that you get when you enjoy your job and feel you have done it well

K

key /kiː/ *adj* most important

L

labour /ˈleɪbə/ *noun* [U] **1** work, usually of a hard, physical kind: *The company wants to keep down* **labour costs**. **2** workers, when thought of as a group

launch /lɔːntʃ/ *verb* to make a new product available to the public for the first time

legal /ˈliːgl/ *adj* allowed by law (opposite: **illegal**)

lifestyle /ˈlaɪfstaɪl/ *noun* [C] the way in which a person or a group of people lives and works

line /laɪn/ *noun* [C] a telephone connection; a particular telephone number

loan /ləʊn/ *noun* [C] an amount of money that sb/a bank, etc. lends you

local economy /ˌləʊkl ɪˈkɒnəmi/ *noun* [C] the operation of a country's or region's money supply, commercial activities and industry

logo /ˈləʊgəʊ/ *noun* [C] a printed symbol or design that a company or organization uses as its special sign

look after sb/sth *phrasal verb* to be responsible for or take care of sb/sth

loss /lɒs/ *noun* [C] money that has been lost by a business or an organization

loyal /ˈlɔɪəl/ *adj* not changing in your friendship or beliefs

lunch break /ˈlʌntʃ breɪk/ *noun* [C] the time around the middle of the day when you stop work or school to eat your lunch

M

mailshot /ˈmeɪlʃɒt/ *noun* [C] advertising or information that is sent to a large number of people at the same time by post

maintain /meɪnˈteɪn/ *verb* to look after sth and keep it in good condition by checking and repairing it regularly

majority /məˈdʒɒrəti/ *noun* [C] (**majority of sb/sth**) the largest number or part of a group of people or things

manage /ˈmænɪdʒ/ *verb* to be in charge of or control of sb/sth

manager /ˈmænɪdʒə/ *noun* [C] a person who is in charge of running a business, a shop or a similar organization or part of one

managing director /ˌmænɪdʒɪŋ dəˈrektə; daɪ-, dɪ-/ *noun* [C] (*abbr* **MD**) (especially Brit) the person who is in charge of a business

manufacture /ˌmænjuˈfæktʃə/ *verb* to make sth in large quantities using machines ➤ **manufacturing** /ˌmænjuˈfæktʃərɪŋ/ *noun* [U]

market¹ /ˈmɑːkɪt/ *noun* [C] (**a market (for sth)**) business or commercial activity; the amount of buying and selling of a particular type of goods

market² /ˈmɑːkɪt/ *verb* to sell a product with the help of advertising ➤ **marketing** /ˈmɑːkɪtɪŋ/ *noun* [U]

market price /ˌmɑːkɪt ˈpraɪs/ *noun* [C] the price that people are willing to pay for sth at a particular time

market research /ˌmɑːkɪt rɪˈsɜːtʃ; ˈrɪsɜːtʃ/ *noun* [U] the work of collecting information about what people buy and why

market share /ˌmɑːkɪt ˈʃeə/ *noun* [U, singular] the amount that a company sells of its products or services compared with other companies selling the same things

MD /ˌem ˈdiː/ = Managing Director

member /ˈmembə/ *noun* [C] a person who belongs to a group, a club, an organization, etc. ➤ **membership** /ˈmembəʃɪp/ *noun* [U]

message /ˈmesɪdʒ/ *noun* 1 [C] a written or spoken piece of information that you send to or leave for a person when you cannot speak to him/her 2 [singular] an important idea that an advertisement, a speech, etc. is trying to communicate

method /ˈmeθəd/ *noun* [C] a particular way of doing sth

minutes /ˈmɪnɪts/ *noun* [pl] (the minutes) written notes of what is said and decided at a meeting

motivated /ˈməʊtɪveɪtɪd/ *adj* wanting to do sth, especially sth that involves hard work or effort

multinational /ˌmʌltiˈnæʃnəl/ *noun* [C] a company that does business in several different countries, especially a large and powerful company ➤ **multinational** *adj*

N

need /niːd/ *noun* [C, usually pl] the things that sb/sth must have

negotiate /nɪˈɡəʊʃieɪt/ *verb* (**negotiate (with sb) (for/about sth)**) to talk to sb in order to decide or agree about sth ➤ **negotiator** /nɪˈɡəʊʃieɪtə/ *noun* [C]

negotiation /nɪˌɡəʊʃiˈeɪʃn/ *noun* [C, often pl, U] a formal discussion at which people try to decide or agree sth

O

objective /əbˈdʒektɪv/ *noun* [C] something that you are trying to achieve

operate /ˈɒpəreɪt/ *verb* to make sth work

opportunity /ˌɒpəˈtjuːnəti/ *noun* [C] a chance to do sth that you want to do

order /ˈɔːdə/ *noun* [C] a request asking for sth to be made, supplied or sent

organigram /ɔːˈɡænəɡræm/ *noun* [C] a diagram that shows the relationship between the positions or jobs of the people working in an organization

organize /ˈɔːɡənaɪz/ *verb* to put or arrange things into a system or logical order

overhead projector /ˌəʊvəhed prəˈdʒektə/ *noun* [C] (*abbr* OHP) a piece of equipment that sends (**projects**) an image onto a wall or screen so that people can see it

overseas /ˌəʊvəˈsiːz/ *adj, adv* in, to or from a foreign country, especially one that you have to cross the sea to get to

overtime /ˈəʊvətaɪm/ *noun* [U] time that you spend at work after your usual working hours; the money that you are paid for this

ownership /ˈəʊnəʃɪp/ *noun* [U] the state of owning sth

P

participant /pɑːˈtɪsɪpənt/ *noun* [C] a person who takes part in (= is present at) sth

patent /ˈpætnt; ˈpeɪtnt/ *noun* [C, U] the official right to be the only person to make, use or sell a product or an invention; the document that proves this

pension /ˈpenʃn/ *noun* [C] money that is paid regularly by a government or company to sb who has stopped working (**retired**) because of old age or disability

percentage /pəˈsentɪdʒ/ *noun* [C] the number, amount, rate, etc. of sth, expressed as if it is part of a total which is a hundred; a part or share of a whole

personal statement /ˌpɜːsənl ˈsteɪtmənt/ *noun* [C] (esp US) a description of your education and working life, your abilities and your goals, that you write when you apply for a job, a place at a university, etc.

pie chart /ˈpaɪ tʃɑːt/ *noun* [C] a diagram consisting of a circle divided into parts to show the size of particular parts in relation to the whole

point /pɔɪnt/ *noun* 1 [C] a particular fact, idea or opinion that sb expresses 2 the point [singular] the most important part of what is being said; the main piece of information

point of sale /ˌpɔɪnt əv ˈseɪl/ *noun* [singular] the place where a product is sold ➤ **point-of-sale** *adj*

polite /pəˈlaɪt/ *adj* having good manners, behaving well and showing respect for other people

portable /ˈpɔːtəbl/ *adj* that can be moved around or carried easily

position /pəˈzɪʃn/ *noun* [C] 1 (**a position (on sth)**) what you think about sth; your opinion 2 (formal) a job

post /pəʊst/ *noun* [C] a job

poster /ˈpəʊstə/ *noun* [C] a large printed picture or a notice in a public place, often used to advertise sth

power /ˈpaʊə/ *verb* to supply energy to sth to make it work

preparation /ˌprepəˈreɪʃn/ *noun* [U] the act or process of getting ready for sth or making sth ready

presentation /ˌpreznˈteɪʃn/ *noun* [C] a meeting at which sth, especially a new product or idea, or piece of work, is shown to a group of people

pressure group /ˈpreʃə ɡruːp/ *noun* [C] a group of people who try to influence the government and ordinary people's opinion in order to achieve the action they want, for example a change in the law

price /praɪs/ *noun* [C] the amount of money that you must pay in order to buy sth

priority /praɪˈɒrəti/ *noun* [C] something that you think is more important than other things and should be dealt with first

private health insurance /ˌpraɪvət ˈhelθ ɪnʃʊərəns/ *noun* [C] an arrangement with a company in which you pay them regular amounts of money and they agree to pay for your treatment in a private hospital or with a private doctor if you are ill

procedure /prəˈsiːdʒə/ *noun* [U] the official or formal order or way of doing sth, especially in business

produce /prəˈdjuːs/ *verb* 1 to make sth to be sold, especially in large quantities 2 to grow or make sth by a natural process ➤ **product** /ˈprɒdʌkt/ *noun* [C] something that is grown or produced, usually to sell

producer /prəˈdjuːsə/ *noun* [C] 1 a person, company or country that grows or makes food, goods or materials 2 a person who is in charge of the practical and financial side of making a film or a play

product awareness /ˌprɒdʌkt əˈweənəs/ *noun* [U] knowledge of your company's products

product range /ˈprɒdʌkt reɪndʒ/ *noun* [C] a set of products of a particular type

production /prəˈdʌkʃn/ *noun* [U] the department in a company responsible for growing or making food, goods or materials

productivity /ˌprɒdʌkˈtɪvəti/ *noun* [U] the speed at which a worker or a company or a country produces goods, and the amount produced, compared with how much time, work and money is needed to produce them

professional[1] /prəˈfeʃənl/ *adj* 1 doing sth in a way that shows skill, training or care 2 suitable or appropriate for sb working in a particular profession

professional[2] /prəˈfeʃənl/ *noun* [C] a person who does a job that needs special training and a high level of education

profit /ˈprɒfɪt/ *noun* [C, U] the money that you make when you sell sth for more than it cost you

profit share /'prɒfɪt ʃeə/ *noun* [C] a system in some companies in which the profit the company has made, for example in one year, is shared out between its directors, shareholders, etc.

profitable /'prɒfɪtəbl/ *adj* that makes money

program /'prəʊgræm/ *noun* [C] a set of instructions that are given to a computer to make it do a particular task

project /'prɒdʒekt/ *noun* [C] a piece of work, often involving many people, that is planned and organized carefully

promotion /prə'məʊʃn/ *noun* 1 [C, U] a move up to a higher position or more important job 2 [U, C] activities done in order to increase the sales of a product or service; a set of advertisements for a particular product or service

proportion /prə'pɔːʃn/ *noun* [C] a part or share of a whole

proposal /prə'pəʊzl/ *noun* [C] a plan that is formally suggested

prospects /'prɒspekts/ *noun* [pl] chances of being successful in the future

prototype /'prəʊtətaɪp/ *noun* [C] the first model or design of sth from which other forms will be developed

purchasing /'pɜːtʃəsɪŋ/ *noun* [U] the department that buys the parts, etc. that the company needs

purpose /'pɜːpəs/ *noun* [C] the aim or intention of sth

Q

qualification /ˌkwɒlɪfɪ'keɪʃn/ *noun* [C] an exam that you have passed or a course of study that you have completed

quality /'kwɒləti/ *noun* 1 [U] a high standard or level 2 [C] a thing that is part of a person's character, especially sth good

questionnaire /ˌkwestʃə'neə/ *noun* [C] a written list of questions that are answered by a number of people so that information can be collected from their answers

R

reasonable /'riːznəbl/ *adj* fair, practical and sensible

record /'rekɔːd/ *noun* [C] (**a record (of sth)**) a written account of what has happened, been done, etc.

recruit /rɪ'kruːt/ *verb* to find new people to join a company

referee /ˌrefə'riː/ *noun* [C] (Brit) a person who gives information about your character and ability, usually in a letter, for example when you are hoping to be chosen for a job

regular /'regjələ/ *adj* done or happening often (opposite: **irregular**)

reliability /rɪˌlaɪə'bɪləti/ *noun* [U] the quality of being able to be trusted to do sth well and to be relied on

rely /rɪ'laɪ/ *verb* (**rely on sb/sth (to do sth)**) to need sb/sth and not be able to live or work properly without him/her/it

report /rɪ'pɔːt/ *noun* [C] a written or spoken description of what you have seen, heard, done, studied, etc.

represent /ˌreprɪ'zent/ *verb* to act or speak in sb else's place or for a group of people

research /rɪ'sɜːtʃ; 'riːsɜːtʃ/ *noun* [U] a detailed and careful study of sth to find out more information about it

research and development /rɪˌsɜːtʃ ən dɪ'veləpmənt/ *noun* [U] (*abbr* **R & D**) the department in a company whose job is to try to find new products or to improve existing ones

resourceful /rɪ'sɔːsfl/ *adj* good at finding ways of doing things and solving problems, etc.
  ➤ **resourcefulness** /rɪ'sɔːsflnəs/ *noun* [U]

respect /rɪ'spekt/ *noun* [U] the feeling that you have when you admire or have a high opinion of sb/sth

responsible /rɪ'spɒnsəbl/ *adj* 1 (**responsible for doing sth**) having the job or duty of dealing with sb/sth, so that is your fault if sth goes wrong 2 (**responsible (to sb/sth)**) having to report to sb/sth with authority, or to sb you are working for ➤ **responsibility** /rɪˌspɒnsə'bɪləti/ *noun* [U,C]

result /rɪ'zʌlt/ *noun* [C] the final situation at the end of a series of actions

revenue /'revənjuː/ *noun* [U, pl] money regularly received by a government, company, etc

reward /rɪ'wɔːd/ *noun* [C] a thing that you are given because you have done sth good, worked hard, etc.

rise /raɪz/ *verb* to move upwards; to become higher, stronger or to increase ➤ **rise** *noun* [C] (**a rise (in sth)**)

role /rəʊl/ *noun* [C] the position or function of sb/sth in a particular situation

routine /ruː'tiːn/ *noun* [C, U] the usual order and way in which you regularly do things

run /rʌn/ *verb* 1 to be in charge of a business, etc.; to manage sth 2 (**run on sth**) to make sth operate or work

S

salary /'sæləri/ *noun* [C,U] the money that a person receives (usually every month) for the work he/she has done

sales /seɪlz/ *noun* [pl] the number of items sold

sales and marketing /ˌseɪlz ən 'mɑːkɪtɪŋ/ *noun* [C] the department in a company that deals with selling and advertising its products

sample /'sɑːmpl/ *noun* [C] a small amount or example of sth that can be looked at or tried to see what it is like

schedule /'ʃedjuːl/ *noun* [C] a plan of things that will happen or of work that must be done

screen /skriːn/ *noun* [C] the glass surface of a television or computer where the picture or information appears

sensor /'sensə/ *noun* [C] a device that can react to light, heat, etc. in order to make a machine, etc. do sth or show sth

service /'sɜːvɪs/ *noun* [C,U] a business whose work involves doing sth for customers but not producing goods; the work that such a business does

set (sth) up *phrasal verb* to start a business, an organization, system, etc.

shake hands (with sb)/shake sb by the hand *idiom* to take sb's hand in yours and move it up and down (when you meet sb, to show you have agreed on sth, etc.)

share[1] /ʃeə/ *verb* 1 to divide sth between two or more people 2 to tell sb about sth; to allow sb to know sth

share[2] /ʃeə/ *noun* 1 [C, usually singular] one part of sth that is divided between two or more people 2 [C, usually pl] one of many equal parts into which the value of a company is divided and which can be sold to people who want to own part of the company

shareholder /'ʃeəhəʊldə/ *noun* [C] a person who owns part of company and receives part of the company's profits

slide /slaɪd/ *noun* [C] a small piece of photographic film in a plastic or cardboard frame

small talk /'smɔːl tɔːk/ *noun* [U] polite conversation, for example at a party, about unimportant things

social life /'səʊʃl ˌlaɪf/ *noun* [C] your free time that you spend outside work doing things for pleasure, usually with other people

software /ˈsɒftweə/ *noun* [U] the programs and other operating information used by a computer

sound recordist /ˈsaʊnd rɪkɔːdɪst/ *noun* [C] a person who works in a recording or film studio and whose job is to control the levels and balance of sound being recorded

spell check /ˈspel tʃek/ *noun* [C] a computer program that checks your writing to see if your spelling (= the way you have written the words) is correct

staff /stɑːf/ *noun* [C, U] the group of people who work for a particular company

stamina /ˈstæmɪnə/ *noun* [U] the ability to do sth that involves a lot of physical or mental effort for a long time

state /steɪt/ *verb* to say or write sth, especially formally ➤ **statement** /ˈsteɪtmənt/ *noun* [C]

steer /stɪə/ *verb* to make sb/sth move in a particular direction

strategy /ˈstrætədʒi/ *noun* 1 [C] a plan that you use in order to achieve sth 2 [U] the process of planning sth or carrying out a plan in a skilful way

stressed /strest/ *adj* too anxious and tired to be able to relax

stressful /ˈstresfl/ *adj* causing worry and pressure

structure /ˈstrʌktʃə/ *noun* [C] the way that the parts of sth are put together and organized

studio /ˈstjuːdiəʊ/ *noun* [C] 1 a place where films are made or produced 2 a company that makes films

subject /ˈsʌbdʒɪkt/ *noun* [C] a thing or person that is being discussed, described or dealt with

subject line /ˈsʌbdʒɪkt laɪn/ *noun* [C] the line at the top of an e-mail where there is space for you to put the name of the person or thing that is being considered or talked about

subsidiary /səbˈsɪdiəri/ *noun* [C] a business company that belongs to and is controlled by another larger company

subsidized /ˈsʌbsɪdaɪzd/ *adj* partly paid for by the government, the company you work for, etc. in order to keep the price low

succeed /səkˈsiːd/ *verb* to manage to achieve what you want; to do well

successful /səkˈsesfl/ *adj* having achieved what you wanted; having become popular, rich, famous, etc.

summary /ˈsʌməri/ *noun* [C] a short description of the main ideas or points of sth but without any details

supplier /səˈplaɪə/ *noun* [C] a person or a company that provides sb/sth with the things that he/she/it needs or wants

supply /səˈplaɪ/ *noun* [C,U] a store or amount of sth that is provided or available to be used; the act of supplying sth

support /səˈpɔːt/ *noun* [U] help and encouragement that you give to sb/sth because you want him/her/it to be successful ➤ **supportive** /səˈpɔːtɪv/ *adj* giving help or encouragement

survey /ˈsɜːveɪ/ *noun* [C] the study of the opinions, behaviour, etc. of a group of people

T

target market /ˌtɑːgɪt ˈmɑːkɪt/ *noun* [C] the particular group of people that a product, etc. is aimed at

tax /tæks/ *noun* [C,U] the money that you have to pay to the government so that it can provide public services

team /tiːm/ *noun* [C] a group of people who work together

telesales /ˈteliseɪlz/ *noun* [U] a method of selling things and taking orders for sales by telephone

title /ˈtaɪtl/ *noun* [C] a word that shows a person's position, profession, etc.

tone /təʊn/ *noun* [C] the general quality or style of sth

track /træk/ *noun* [C] a circular belt of metal, rubber, etc. around the wheels of a large vehicle that allows it to move over the ground

trade /treɪd/ *noun* [U] the buying or selling of goods or services between people or countries

trainee /ˌtreɪˈniː/ *noun* [C] a person who is learning how to do a particular job

training /ˈtreɪnɪŋ/ *noun* [U] the process of learning the skills that you need in order to do a job

training course /ˈtreɪnɪŋ kɔːs/ *noun* [C] a series of classes, etc., in which you learn a skill or how to do a particular task

translate /trænsˈleɪt; trænz-/ *verb* to change sth written or spoken from one language into another ➤ **translator** /trænsˈleɪtə; trænz-/ *noun* [C]

transmit /trænsˈmɪt; trænz-/ *verb* to send out radio or television programmes, electronic signals, etc.

travel allowance /ˈtrævl əlaʊəns/ *noun* [C] an amount of money that is given to an employee to cover the cost of journeys to and from work, business travel, etc.

trend /trend/ *noun* [C] (**a trend (towards sth)**) a general change or development

turn /tɜːn/ *noun* [C, usually singular] a time when sb in a group of people should or is allowed to do sth

twice /twaɪs/ *adv* double in quantity, speed, etc.

U

unethical /ʌnˈeθɪkl/ *adj* not morally acceptable

unique /juˈniːk/ *adj* very special or unusual

unselfish /ʌnˈselfɪʃ/ *adj* giving more time or importance to other people's needs, wishes, etc. than to your own

USP /ˌjuː es ˈpiː/ *noun* [C] abbreviation for 'unique selling point'; something that makes one product more desirable to buyers because no other product does anything similar

V

values /ˈvæljuːz/ *noun* [pl] beliefs about what is the right and wrong way for people to behave; moral principles

variable /ˈveəriəbl/ *adj* not staying the same; changing or likely to change: *variable costs*

venue /ˈvenjuː/ *noun* [C] the place where people meet for an organized event, for example a concert, sporting event or a conference

vice-president /ˌvaɪs ˈprezɪdənt/ *noun* [C] (*abbr* **VP**) (especially US) a person in charge of a particular part of a business company

video camera /ˈvɪdiəʊ kæmərə/ *noun* [C] a special camera for making video films

voluntary work /ˈvɒləntri wɜːk/ *noun* [U] work that is done without payment, for a charity, etc.

VP /ˌviː ˈpiː/ = Vice-President

W

website /ˈwebsaɪt/ *noun* [C] a place connected to the Internet, where a company, an organization, etc. puts information that can be found on the World Wide Web

willing /ˈwɪlɪŋ/ *adj* happy to do sth; having no reason for not doing sth

wiring /ˈwaɪərɪŋ/ *noun* [U] the system of wires that is used for supplying electricity to a building or machine

working hours /ˈwɜːkɪŋ aʊəz/ *noun* [pl] the number of hours in the week that you spend doing your job

worthwhile /ˌwɜːθˈwaɪl/ *adj* enjoyable, useful and satisfying enough to be worth the effort